INTELLECTUAL PROPERTY RIGHTS OF FARMERS

INTELLECTUAL PROPERTY RIGHTS OF FARMERS

DR. PREM KUMAR AGARWAL
Head of the Department
Law Section
Hooghly Mohsin College
Chinsurah, Hooghly (W.B.)
Ex. WBCS (Judicial)

DEEP & DEEP PUBLICATIONS PVT. LTD.
F-159, Rajouri Garden, New Delhi - 110 027

INTELLECTUAL PROPERTY RIGHTS OF FARMERS

ISBN 978-81-8450-399-9

Typeset by RAHUL COMPOSERS
358, Pocket-B, Phase-2, Sector-16B, Dwarka, New Delhi - 110 075

Printed in India at MAYUR ENTERPRISES
WZ Plot No. 3, Gujjar Market, Tihar Village, New Delhi - 110 018

Published by DEEP & DEEP PUBLICATIONS PVT. LTD.
F-159, Rajouri Garden, New Delhi - 110 027 • Phone : 25435369, 25440916
E-mail : ddpubs@gmail.com • ddpbooks@yahoo.co.in
Showroom :
2/13, Ansari Road, Daryaganj, New Delhi - 110 002 • Telefax : 23245122

Contents

Acknowledgements

It is a matter of great pleasure to express my profound gratitude to Prof. (Dr.) Shiv Sahai Singh, Senior Professor of Law, The University of Burdwan, Burdwan, West Bengal who has supervised this project and guided me in pursuing this study to its socio-legal end, despite his busy schedule. I take this opportunity to express my sincere indebtedness to Prof. (Dr.) S.S. Singh for devoting his valuable time for going through the draft and suggesting a number of amendments in it.

I express my gratitude to The Head of The Department of Law, Dr. Manik Chakraborty and ex-head of The Department Dr. S.K. Sadhu. I express my respect to Dr. A.H. Mondal (Ret. Prof.) and Dr. M. Momin, Reader in Law, Dr. Dipak Das, Dr. Sanjeev Kumar Tiwari, Lecturers in Law for their valuable suggestions during the completion of the work. I would like to record my sincere thanks to Principal, Hooghly Mohsin College, Chinsurah and all my colleagues in the college for constant encouragement. My heartfelt thanks are due to Mr. Kankan Choudhury, Librarian, Law Library and other staff of the Library, Hooghly Mohsin College. I would also like to thank Mr. Golam Ambia, Ex-Librarian, Department of Law, Burdwan University and all others of the Department for their sincere cooperation. I will be failing in my duty if I do not express my gratitude to Dr. Philippe Cullet of the School of Oriental and African Studies, London, Dr. Sudhir Kochar of PUSA, New Delhi for their help.

My humble acknowledgement is due to the authorities and staffs of the Library of Indian Law Institute, New Delhi, The Indian Society of International Law, New Delhi, Ministry of Human Resource Development, Govt. of India, Ministry of Law and Justice, Government of India, Library of Supreme Court, New Delhi, IIPA, New Delhi, USIS, British Council Library, National Library, The Library of The WB National University of Juridical Sciences, Kolkata and Central Library of Burdwan University for their help in this academic endeavour.

I will be failing in my duty if I do not express my gratitude and gratefulness to my parents. My Father Shri Kailash Chandra Agarwal and Mother Smt. Radha Devi Agarwal have been constant source of inspiration in all my academic pursuits. The credit of providing a congenial atmosphere to complete the study at home goes to my wife Smt. Sheelam Agarwal. Whenever I was wanting in energy my son Umang and daughter Sneha recharged me with their affection and love.

In completing this study many known and unknown persons have guided, helped and assisted me. Their suggestions have benefited me in a number of ways. I am grateful to all of them.

Ultimately, the author would like to record his appreciation for the efforts of M/s. Deep and Deep Publications (P) Ltd., New Delhi, who made the arduous business of seeing it through the press as smoothly as possible.

PREM KUMAR AGARWAL

Abbreviations

CCMB — The Centre for Cellular and Molecular Biology
CBD — Convention on Biological Diversity
CGIAR — The Consultative Group on International Agricultural Research
CGRFA — Commission on Genetic Resources for Food and Agriculture
COP — Conference of the Parties
CSO — Civil Society Organisation
CTE — Committee on Trade and Environment
DNA — Deoxyribonucleic Acid
DUS — Distinct, Uniform and Stable
ECOSOC — Economic and Social Council
EMR — Exclusive Marketing Right
EPC — European Patent Convention
EPO — European Patent Office
EST — Expressed Sequence Tags
EU — European Union
FAO — Food and Agricultural Organisation
GATT — General Agreement on Tariffs and Trade
GIFTS — Germplasm, Information, Funds, Technologies and System
GMO — Genetically Modified Organisms
IPCU — International Patent Classification Union

IPDL	—	Intellectual Property Digital Libraries
IPR	—	Intellectual Property Rights
JOPAL	—	Journal of Patent Associated Literature
LDC	—	Least Developed Countries
MFN	—	Most Favoured Nations
MTA	—	Material Transfer Agreement
MNC	—	Multi National Corporation
NGO	—	Non-Government Organisation
NIF	—	National Innovation Foundation
NIH	—	National Institute of Health
OAU	—	Organization of African Unity
OJEPO	—	Official Journal of the European Patent Organisation
PBR	—	Plant Breeders' Rights
PGR	—	Plant Genetic Resources
PGRFA	—	Plant Genetic Resources For Food and Agriculture
PTO	—	Patent and Trademark Office
PVPC	—	Plant Variety Protection Certificates
RAFI	—	Rural Advancement Foundation International
SAARC	—	South Asia Association for Regional Cooperation
SADC	—	Southern Africa Development Cooperation
SCIT	—	Standing Committee on Information Technology
SCP	—	Standing Committee on the Law Patents
SNP	—	Single Nucleotide Polymorphisms
SPLT	—	Substantive Patent Law Treaty
SRISTI	—	Society for Research and Initiatives for Sustainable Technologies and Institutions
TIFAC	—	Technology Information Forecasting and Assessment Council
TKDL	—	Traditional Knowledge Digital Libraries

TKRC	—	Traditional Knowledge Resources Classification
TNC	—	Trans National Corporation
TRIPS	—	Trade Related Intellectual Property Rights
USC	—	United States Code
UNCTAD	—	United Nations Conference on Trade and Development
UNDP	—	United Nations Development Programme
UPOV	—	Union International Pour Law Protection Des Obtentions Vegetables (International Union for the Protection of New Varieties of Plants)
USDAER	—	US Department of Agriculture Economics Research Service
USPTO	—	US Patent and Trademark Office
WHO	—	World Health Organisation
WIPO	—	World Intellectual Property Organisation
WTO	—	World Trade Organisation

1

Introduction

"The crossing of wild wheat goat grass around 8000 B.C. produced a fertile hybrid called *emmer. Emmer* spread naturally by being broadcast in the wind and a further cross of emmer and another natural goat grass created the bread wheat with its plump of 42 chromosomes. This wheat had its grain ear tightly covered with husk. It could not crack by itself. This bread wheat needed an agent to open its ear so that it can be sown and spread. Man has a wheat he lives by, but the wheat also thinks that man has been made for wheat because only so can it be propagated. The life of each man and plant depended on the other. It is a true fairy tale of genetics, as if the coming of civilisation has been blessed in advance by the spirit of Mendel."—The Brownskian approach to bio-technology by D.M. Balasubramanium of The Centre for Cellular and Molecular Biology (C.C.M.B)[1] vividly depicts the tryst of man and nature right from the dawn of creation. Among all the species that adore the globe *homo sapiens* are outstanding because of possessing 'intellect' with which man has

1. S. Biswasnathan, C. Parmar, 'A Biotechnology Story' : *EPW,* July 6th, 2002.

conquered ravages of nature and harnessed the natural forces for his own comfort and well-being. The role of the power of the human mind is now being acknowledged as a major wealth creator in every economy.

To an increasing degree knowledge rather than labour or conventional property is becoming constitutive for economic and social activities. Knowledge has become the source of economic growth and competitive advantage among firms, society and regions of the world. The developments allow us to speak of the transformation of modern industrial society into a *knowledge society*. It represents a social and economic world in which more and more things are "made" to happen, rather than a social reality in which things simply "happen".

Innovation is the key for the production as well as processing of knowledge. A nation's ability to convert knowledge into wealth and social good through the process of innovation will determine its future.

In this context, issues of generation, valuation, protection and exploitation of intellectual property are becoming critically important all around the world. Exponential growth of scientific knowledge, increasing demand for new forms of IPR protection as well as access to IP-related information, increasing dominance of the new knowledge economy over the old 'brick and mortar' economy, complexities linked to IP in traditional knowledge, community knowledge and animate objects will pose a challenge in setting the new 21st century IP agenda.[2]

The economic dynamics and impacts of the myriad activities collectively referred to as 'biotechnology' portend to offer vast employment and commercial benefits. It is thus not surprising that many pundits in the private sector wax enthusiastically about the potential of this new 'frontier' of research if market forces are allowed to fuel investments and competition, unbridled to the extent possible by government hands. Yet, the nature of the technology, e.g. potentially changing conceptions of ourselves permitting the development

2. R.A. Mashelkar, 'Intellectual Property Rights and The Third World', *Journal of Intellectual Property Rights,* Vol. 7, July, 2002.

of techniques which no one knows with certainty what the ecological effects might be, etc. have led to legitimate public debates.

Central to these are deeper concerns regarding ownership between biotechnology as a public good or as a private assets. Debate over ownership typically pivots on questions about property rights, public access, and the equitable distribution of benefits derived from advances in bio-techniques. Of course, prevailing legal conception of property and notions of ownership include the right of possession, use, management, income, security, transmissibility and exclusivity. In other words a public fear is that governments will loose control of this transformative and soon-to-be pervasive technology.

Ethical concerns with biotechnology clearly cover a broad swath. If one could try to typify these, a spectrum might range form moral issues (in which case cloning and other bio-techniques is felt to put 'Man' in place of 'God'), to basic anti-technology sentiments, to a fear of the unknown or more precisely, to a sense that bio-technology will increase uncertainty and thus public risk, to a core anti-capitalist or anti-corporatist reaction—particularly when it is felt or shown either that there is 'excessive' profit taking in certain bio-technology sector (e.g. MNC seed monopoly) or that the benefits derived from bio-technology in terms of nutrition, agriculture and health are not only not being distributed to developing world but are actually having negative impacts on these impoverished regions. Concern with risk management is probably the most legitimate of these, but these together merely point to the dynamic interface between policy, business and society with this evolving technology. They certainly point to the environment with in which policy-makers must work. *This policy has to be reflected in law. Thus the ideal law should try to foster a symbiotic social contract between science and society. In fact, justice and science must combine in the idea of sustainability. Bio-technology has to become only one example of these axiomatic concepts through proper Jurisprudence.*

The post-Vienna legal phase is remarkably known for revolutionary changes across the globe wherein the doctrinaire limits of international and municipal law has been blurred.[3] In the arena of Intellectual Property Rights (IPR) this seems more true because fresh spate of statutory activism making trade international in character now seems to determine the relationship among the comity of nations. The onset of World Trade Organisation (WTO) jurisprudence (often described as Pro-North Jurisprudence) owes its genesis to Bretton Wood Conference, 1944, General Agreement On Trade and Tariffs (GATT), Arthur Dunkel Draft, Uruguay Round, and Marrakesh Agreement. The Bretton Wood Conference marked the beginning of a new world trade order which triggered economic changes and paradigm shift. This paved the way for preparation of Dunkel Draft eventuating in the Uruguay Round and Marrakesh Agreement.[4] The major thrust has been the creation of world-wide market grab system under the exuberance of globalization, liberalization and privatization. The GATT was tuned in such a way that it became instrumentality for the implementation of planetary business agenda.

The post-GATT-ised legal ordering is remarkably known for much publicized and debatable conclusion of Trade Related Aspect of Intellectual Property Rights (TRIPS) and creation of WTO. These jurisprudential polemics soon evoked fierce scrutiny.[5] At home, in some quarter, it is dubbed as 'bleeding operation with the dubious promise of benign global competition', '*de facto* nullity of constitutional goal of social welfare' and 'contra-constitutional coup'.[6] Since India has become a member of WTO it indulged into massive rehabilitation and fundamental mutation of IPR regime. In

---

3. Upendra Baxi, 'Environmental Teaching and Research In Universities', in Association of Indian Universities (ed.) *Environmental Challenges and the Universities,* 44 (1994).
4. Rajeev Dhavan and Maya Prabhu, 'Patent Monopolies and Free Trade : Basic Contradiction in Dunkel Draft', XXXVII (2), *The Journal of Indian Law Institute,* 195-208 (1995).
5. M.R. Agosin *et al.,* Developing Countries and the Uruguay Round : An Evaluation And Issues For The 'Future', in United Nations Conference on Trade and Development Report (1995).
6. V.R. Krishna Iyer, GATT, TRIPS and Patent Law-I, *The Hindu Daily : New Delhi Edition,* Sept. 11, 2000, p. BS-4.

view of nearing deadline of transitional phase and evaporation of euphoria of most favored nations (MFN), our legislatures swung into action by proposing three Bills for the enactment in the Parliament. Two of the Bills (now Acts), *The Protection of plant Varieties and Farmers' Right Act and Patent (Amendment) Act* constitutes India's response to *TRIPS Agreement. The Biological Diversity Act* on the other hand seeks to implement the mandate of *U.N. Convention on Biological Diversity, 1992 (CBD)*. The three Acts have their own distinct focus but they share in common an attempt to define property rights over biological resources or inventions related to bio-diversity. The allocation of real and intellectual property rights over biological resources has become a matter of great concern.[7] The unique dovetailing of natural resources with global trade law has been a cause of great discontentment as the country never encountered such problem in spite of the fact that its patent legislation has stood the test of time and acclaimed far and wide. The insurmountable pressure of WTO, growing menace of bio-piracy, gradual commodification of natural agricultural and environmental resources and prevalent apathy and ignorance about the digitization of the indigenous knowledge and traditional practices are perceived as 're-colonization in the making', 'global village-global tillage' agenda and jettisoning of country's basic welfare obligation. Under this backdrop the study subsumes the community of concerns and assesses the potential and portent of TRIPS Agreement in strategizing an effective *sui generis* system of protection of plant variety, farmers and breeders' right, bio-diversity, traditional knowledge, etc.

After the assumption of original membership of WTO India is on the threshold of revamping the IPR laws. Some of the important radical changes effectuated to fulfil the TRIPS mandate include:

- A system for filing and handling product patent applications for pharmaceutical and agriculture chemical products and the granting of Exclusive

7. Philippe Cullet, 'Bill On IPRs I : Bio-Diversity Legislation Reflects India's Obligation', *The Hindu Daily*, Feb. 22, 2001, BS-4.

marketing rights (EMRs) (to be implemented as of 1 January 1995; adopted in March 1999);

- The elimination of any restriction on the granting of product patents (as of 1 January, 2000) except for product patents on pharmaceutical and agricultural chemical products (where restrictions can remain until 1 January, 2005);
- The elimination of restrictions on patentable subject matter such as the current exclusion of methods of agriculture or horticulture (as of 1 January, 2000);
- The lengthening of patent duration to twenty years, from the current fourteen years, and seven years for food and pharmaceuticals (as of 1 January, 2000);[8]
- Restrictions and modifications concerning compulsory licensing. Licenses of right and the right of revocation (as of 1 January, 2000); and
- The adoption of a legal regime for the protection of plant varieties (as of 1 January, 2000). This takes the form of a Plant Variety Protection Act.[9]

The operational strategy has been devised into two phases. The first phase of reform, which encompassed provisions for filing product patent and grant of exclusive marketing right, is already over. The second phase reforms subsume implications on the overall growth of pharmaceutical industry, share of foreign and domestic investment, research and development and international trade mechanism.[10] The fundamental mutation of Indian Patent Act is hailed and assailed. One set of opinions runs the Patent Act is development-oriented and patriotically processed statute. It has been passed after a meaningful debate and thorough study and proved a national triumph for commerce and

8. Philipe Cullet, 'Revision of the TRIPS Agreement Concerning the Protection of Plant Varieties : Lessons from India Concerning the Development of A Sui Generis System', 2(4) *The Journal of World Intellectual Property,* 625 (1999).
9. *Id.,* at 626.
10. M.D. Nair, 'Amendment to Patent Act : Option Under TRIPS', *The Hindu Daily,* March 8, 2001, p. BS-3.

manufacturer alike.[11] Those who assailed revolution in the western world witnessed very little impact on industrial scene particularly in the innovation dependent industrial segment.[12] In the midst of claims and counter-claims the leeway and loopholes of TRIPS needs to be examined logically. Unlike the general perception the Agreement provides considerable maneuvering to make it developing country friendly. A perusal of some of the provisions of TRIPS supports this view. Any developing country member which is in the process of transformation from a centrally planned into a market-free enterprise economy and which is undertaking structural reform of intellectual property system and facing special problems in preparation and implementation of intellectual property laws, may benefit or entitled for delay.[13] In view of special needs and requirement in least developed countries, their economic, financial and administrative constraints and their need for flexibility to create a viable technological base, such member shall not be required to apply to the provisions of this agreement, other than Articles 3, 4 and 5 for a period of ten years.[14] Further latitude is granted under the Agreement which is an armory in hands of municipal legislature to safeguard the national interests. It runs as under:

Member-states may exclude from patentability inventions, the prevention within their territory of the commercial exploitation of which is necessary to protect public order or morality, including to protect human, animal or plant life or health or to avoid serious prejudice to the environment, provided that such exclusion is not made merely because the exploitation is prohibited by domestic law.[15]

Member-states may also exclude from patentability the diagnostic, therapeutic and surgical methods for the treatment

---

11. Rajeev Dhavan, Lindsay Harris and Gopal Jain, 'Power Without Responsibility : On Aspect of the Indian Patents Legislation', XXXIII (1), *The Journal of Indian Law Institute*, 2-6 (1991).
12. *Supra* note 10.
13. Article 65(20) (30), *The Trade Related Aspects of Intellectual Property Rights*, 1995.
14. *Id.*, Article 66(1).
15. *Id.*, Article 27(2).

of humans and animals *vis-a-vis* plants and animals other than micro-organism and essentially biological processes for the production of plants or animals other than non-biological and micro-biological processes. However, the members shall provide for the protection of plants varieties either by the patent or by effective *sui generis* system or by any combination thereof.[16]

This constitutes one of the few areas where India is conferred some margin of appreciation in devising protective *sui generis* system. Some countries in the South American region have made use of these provisions to bring in restrictions on patentability in their national patent laws. As far as India is concerned, in view of the need to protect some indigenous systems, it may have been important to have a wider rather than a restrictive interpretation of Article 27.3(a) to include indigenous products and knowledge bases.[17] A matter of great concern to India is the one related to the provisions for granting patents for discovering new uses for known molecules or products. While India wants protection of its bio-assets from exploitation through second use patents by third parties, it should also consider the possibility of taking patents on new uses for existing products out of its own R & D efforts. TRIPS is silent on this issue. Implying that countries are free to decide for themselves whether it is advantageous for them to allow filing and grant of utility patents, like in the U.S.[18]

The protection of plant variety, farmers and breeders tights derives its life breath and sustenance from Union International Pour Law Protection Des Obtentions Vegetables or International Union for the Protection of new Varieties of Plants or UPOV Convention. The Convention was signed in Paris in 1961 and enforced in 1968. It was put to revision in 1972, 1978 and 1991. It ensures protection to plant variety and grant exclusive property right on DUS Criteria distinct, uniform and stable. For three decades (1961-1991), UPOV

16. *Id.*, Article 27(3).
17. *Supra* note 10.
18. *Ibid.*

Convention has been granting following privileges/ exemptions:

(i) Breeder exemptions, which allowed the breeders to use the protected varieties for research purposes and for breeding new varieties, and

(ii) Farmers' privilege, which allowed the farmers to use their own harvested material of the protected variety for sowing the next crop on their own farm.

The Convention constitutes an alternative to patents insofar as plant breeders' rights provide slightly weaker rights to commercial breeders. However, it does not recognize farmers as breeders, and rights over varieties. *On the whole, the current international legal framework favors the appropriation of biological resources and related knowledge through sovereign rights and private property rights*. It generally seeks to increase incentives for the commercial exploitation of these resources and knowledge. One of the consequences is that the role of common property rights which are still very important in many rural communities for the fulfilment of basic food and health needs is progressively side-lined. It thus provides a partial framework which is inherently of granting rights to farmer breeders despite the fact that an overwhelming majority of seeds planted in India are farm-saved seeds. Since TRIPS leaves member-states to choose their own system of plant varieties protection, it is evident that countries such as India where agriculture provides employment to at least two-thirds of the working population should adopt a system adapted to their own needs and requirements, something that UPOV can not achieve.

India's concern for a comprehensive legislation bears legitimacy because it is one of the twelve mega diversity regions of the world and constitutes seven percent of world's flora.[19] The government has thrashed out Bio-diversity Policy which broadly encapsulates survey of bio-diversity, national

19. Md. Zafar Mahfooz Nomani, 'Laws and Flaws Relating to Conservation of Biological Diversity : A Kaleidoscopic View', (2000) 2, *The Company Law Journal*, pp. 17-22.

data base, *in-situ* and *ex-situ* conservation, sustainable utilization, indigenous knowledge systems, benefit sharing, people's participation, international cooperation, research, education, training and extension. Falling in line with BD Policy *The Biological Diversity* Act, 2002 entails information sharing system, chronicling sustainable use and community benefit sharing.[20] The twin provisions envisaged under CBD viz.; right to sovereignty and equitable sharing of benefits among indigenous communities needs urgent restructuring in IPR regime because of prevalent unethical dichotomies in recognition-reward system. The conflicting sets of legal moralities was detected after one year of conclusion of CBD because India become signatory to WTO Agreement in 1995. Thus, trading interests reflected in WTO have over ridden two basic assumptions, which are fundamental to CBD. Firstly, IPR is a matter of national sovereignty and policy because it establishes monopolies and monopolies are de facto dangerous Secondly, life forms are part of public domain. Subjecting the ecological and cultural heritage of indigenous communities to the legal regime of commercial monopoly right under TRIPS will place them in serious jeopardy.

Since TRIPS mandates IPR could be universally applied to all technologies, bio-diversity, genetic resources and plant variety automatically becomes subject to patent either under global patent regime or *sui generis* national system. It was possible for India to insist that the both TRIPS and the CBD, one insisting on conformity and other on diversity, can not be right at the same time. Unfortunately, such arguments have not been fruitfully deployed by the Indian governments in international negotiations to counter patentability.[21] Therefore, the Bio-diversity Act is seen with great expectations and an

20. Md. Zafar Mahfooz Nomani, 'Environment Agriculture and Challenges of Biopiracy: A Blue Print of Indian Sui-Generis Legal Order'. Paper presented in the International Conference on Environment Agriculture and Poverty, Department of Geography, A.M.U., Aligarh, (March 4-5, 2001).
21. *Phillippe Cullet*, 'Intellectual Property Rights: For an Alternative Patent Regime', xvi (21) *The Frontline Magazine*, 91 (1999).

instrument to ward-off some of the deficiencies of PVP & FR Act and IPR regime of India. The Bio-diversity Act has been drafted in response to the Bio-diversity Convention (CBD) and reflects, Government's strong reaction to bio-piracy, illegal application of resource or knowledge and partly to avoidance of a direct confrontation with WTO.[22] However, it does not provide a comprehensive framework for the conservation and sustainable use of biological resources. In fact it focuses on access and assertion of the sovereign rights over natural resources. While the Act focuses on preserving India's interests its main impact within the country will be to concentrate power in the hands of the Government. The Act has logical bearing with PVP & FR Act as it addresses the question of the rights of holders of local knowledge by setting up a system of benefit sharing. It is innovative in so far as it provides that an authority can grant joint ownership of monopoly intellectual property right to the inventor and the authority or to the actual contributors if they can be identified. However, sharing property right is only one of the avenues for the authority to discharge its obligation to determine benefit sharing. Further, it is in the authority's power to allocate right to itself or a contributor such as a farmer contributor and the latter has no right to demand to allocation of property rights. The Act thus accepts the introduction of IPR over bio-diversity as provided for in TRIPS Agreement but does not directly seek to make sure IPRs are subordinated to CBD as provided in the convention.[23]

The Patents Act of 1970 deals with patents in general and is not specifically related to biological resources and patentability of methods of agriculture.[24] In view of WTO-TRIPS mandate the Act has undergone a fundamental change and still awating further amendments. But before finalizing the new Patent Act India should take into account socio-economic

22. Philippe Cullet, 'Bill On IPRs III : Bio-Diversity Bill Insists on Sovereign Rights, *The Hindu Daily,* March 8, 2001, BS-4
23. *Ibid.*
24. Sumam Sahai, 'Indian Patent Act and TRIPS', XXVIII, *The Economic and Political Weekly,* 1495 (1993).

complexities of Indian agro-diversity[25] and leverage and loopholes of TRIPS Agreement.[26] Therefore, the new amendments to *The Patents Act* generally seek to modify the Act to allow compliance with TRIPS. However, the exceptions contained in TRIPS have not necessarily been used to their full extent. *Further, the present Act does not consider at all the impact of the strengthening of patent rights on the realization of fundamental rights such as the right to food and health despite their close links with regard to environmental protection.*[27] Though the Act includes some of the TRIPS exceptions related to environment and health, it generally addresses the question of bio-piracy by imposing the disclosure of the source and geographical origin of biological material used in a patented invention. Further, non-discloser of the geographical origin or the anticipation of the invention in local or indigenous knowledge constitutes grounds for opposing or revoking a patent.

The three Acts generally reflect the trend towards the appropriation by States and private actors of a multiplicity of property rights the gradual dismissal of common property rights regimes and the denial of the principle of free exchange of resources and knowledge as the basic premises for managing genetic resources.[28] The sovereign rights over biological resource is relatively weak and it is likely that main beneficiaries of this regime will be the private sector, local industry and multinational companies.[29] The introduction and strengthening of private property rights constitutes one of the

25. M.S. Swaminathan, 'Agro-bio-diversity and Farmers' Rights' Proceeding of Technical Consultation of Implementation Framework for Farmers' Right, MSSRF, Madras (1996).
26. Vandana Shiva, *Future of Our Seeds, Future of Our Farmers: Agricultural Bio-diversity, Intellectual Property and Farmers' Right.* (1996).
27. Md. Zafar Mahfooz Nomani, 'The Human Right to Environment in India : Legal Percepts and Judicial Doctrines in Critical Perspective', (2000) 5, *The Asia Pacific Journal of Environmental Law,* 113-34.
28. Phillip Cullet, 'Bill on IPRs IV : Concerns with Proposed Law', *The Hindu Daily,* March 15, 2001 p. BS-4.
29. *Ibid.*

most significant elements of the new regime. *However, farmers, local communities and other managers of bio-diversity are not given intellectual property rights to their knowledge. In exchange, the concept of benefit-sharing has been introduced as via-media in a bid to recognize the contribution of these actors while usually denying them property rights.*[30] The three Acts deal in part with the same subject matter. But it is surprising that the bio-diversity Act definition of biological resources does not exclude plant varieties given the existence of a separate plant variety legislation. These overlaps do not stop at the level of definitions. The bio-diversity and plant variety Act which both deal with fundamentally similar issues and subject matters each seek to set-up their own national authority instead of providing a single common body. Further, both adopt benefit-sharing as a compensatory mechanism but they set-up benefit sharing mechanisms that are distinct and unrelated. One provides financial compensation and other property rights. This may lead to considerable difficulties, overlapping mandates and inconsistencies from conceptual to technical implementation issues.[31]

Rest of the study attempts to encapsulate the confluence of the different streams which evolves a new branch of Jurisprudence of Intellectual Property Rights.

As said by Roscoe Pound, the main pillar of the Sociological jurisprudence the State as a juristic person requires to protect social interest. He propounded the theory of social engineering. According to him, every law should ensure the achievement of social fact meaning thereby a social investigation of conflicting interests, preparation of inventory of such interests and to balance and harmonise these conflicting claims and interests, with the aim to build as efficient a structure of the society as possible to ensure the maximum satisfaction of wants with a minimum of friction and waste.[32] Thus, in every civilized society the main function of law has been to reconcile and balance the competing and conflicting interests, i.e., the individual interest and social

30. *Ibid.*
31. *Ibid.*
32. Roscoe Pound : 'An Introduction to Philosophy of Law', 1995, p. 47.

interest in order to achieve maximum satisfaction of the needs of society at the cost of curtailment of minimum freedom of individuals.

That is why the government and its instrument, the law, are keen enough to strike a balance between countervailing forces of TNC/Industry/commercial breeders and farmers—a very important yet a most difficult and delicate task to perform. Further, social justice requires that the state for its own existence owe an obligation to the community to bridge the gap between the two classes and evolve a healthy social order. *It is from this fountain of social justice that the necessity of legal recognition of intellectual contribution of generation of farmers has flown.*

Power to make policy, power to make rules and power to ensure obedience to rules are the powers available to the State machinery to regulate socio-economic relations. As opined by Friedmann,[33] the State as an arbiter in a democratic society has three tasks: the maintenance of a rough balance between contending organized groups and the usually unorganized consumer, the protection of the individual freedom of association and the safeguarding of overriding State interests.

There has been much debate going on, both in national and international spheres, among industrialists, trade unionists, economists, social workers, NGOs, legal and political philosophers, academicians of various disciplines about the implications of globalisation policies for society and economy in general and its impact on agrarian relations in particular. World-wide protests are on rise against the globalisation. The organisations like Asian Social Forum and others are voicing their protests by organizing seminars and symposiums. Demonstrations and protest rallies are being organized at the venues of WTO meetings. The recent Cancum and Hong Kong summits are no exceptions. Developing nations like India, who are pursuing the policies under the threats of trade sanctions, social clauses, consumer boycotts are also gradually realising the relative advantages and disadvantages of global economic policies for developed and

33. W. Friedman, 'Law in a Changing Society', 2nd edn., 1996, pp. 137-38.

developing nations. The failure of Cancum summit of WTO is very significant in this regard. But for the concerted action of the developing countries led by India, the developed nations through WTO would have succeeded in imposing their own action plan meant to further their own interests on the developing nations.

All these developments raise a crucial question whether the Indian legal system can meet the challenges of globalisation and prevent the social tensions that may take place in socio economic relations and to protect the rights of the farmers in order to achieve growth with social justice. The apparent end of a particular legal system is no doubt determined by the dominant political and economic ideology of the society. But we have reached a stage wherein, cutting across all ideological differences, there is a consensus that law should promote social solidarity by furthering wider community interests. This is what Roscoe Pound has characterised as "socialization of law" and others in various ways such as social solidarity, social harmony, social welfare, etc.[34]

As contemplated by Pound[35] and other sociological jurists, Law should be studied in its functional aspect rather than attempting to explain abstractly what law is. There has been a shift in the focus of inquiry from the nature of law to its functions, so how the law is actually working in a given society should be considered to assess its efficacy to meet the existing social and economic conditions and its effectiveness to face the new challenges. This functional attitude helps us to measure legal norms by the extent to which they further or achieve the ends of the given legal order. When the legal system itself is in a state of flux, this approach will enable us to determine whether we are moving in a right direction.

---

34. Dr. A. Jayagovind : 'From Order to Chaos—Some Reflections on International Economic Order'. Paper Presented at 'The Commonwealth Legal Education Association Conference' on 'Economic Policies, Human Rights and The Legal Order' held at Bangalore on 4-6-1993.
35. Roscoe Pound : 'An Introduction to Philosophy of Law', 1995, p. 52.

The legal system in India, so far, has functioned in the context of the ideals of Welfare State, tending to move towards socialism, under a regime of mixed economy with the public sector as the dominant sector, choosing the policy and legislative measures protecting the farmer from the exploitation by all powerful capital and strived to achieve growth coupled with social justice. Now the times have changed. The Government of India is committed to dismantling of state-controlled and regulated economy, and to promote the policies of liberalization, privatization and globalization under the influence, direction and command of the World Bank and International Monetary Fund. The economic reforms announced by the Government have changed the direction of the country from the socialistic pattern to market economy. The shift in Government's IPR policy in tune with on going economic reforms and consequential move to amend IPR laws will have tremendous impact on the agrarian relations, in addition to the impact it will have on the society in general. As a result, the farmers face a crisis with declining protection afforded to them. In this process, the greatest worry now posing to the farmers is the insecurity in the face of monopolization of seed supply by the MNCs. These new issues and concerns create new complexities and challenges leading to crisis in agrarian relations.

The welfare philosophy—a detailed agenda for promotion of social sector Human capital appearing in the preamble and directive principles of the Indian Constitution, is directly linked up with the role of the State in 'Nehruvian' model of development. This model of development was characterized by a highly interventionist State as opposed to laissez faire State,[36] where welfarism was an identified concern and a deep rooted constitutional commitment. However, the introduction of globalisation motivated new economic policy in India, led to a new thinking of the role of the State and develops a need to redefine the role of the State in social, economic and industrial relations fields in the light of Constitutional ethos of

36. Dr. Raghunandha Reddy : 'A Marked Driven Economy : The Constitutional Drift and Paradigm Shift', *Indian Bar Review*, Vol. 29(2), 2002, p. 63.

'socialism', 'social justice' and 'welfare State'. Hence, the questions that naturally arise are: Could the State contract out of its social welfare commitments in the background of ongoing reform process? Are the current economic policies in consonance with the constitutional philosophy? Is globalisation not posing a new challenge to the rights of the farmers and creating new complexities in agrarian relations?

All these issues give rise to fundamental question as to the social, legal and constitutional relevance of the changing role of the State and the consequential shift in its economic policies warranting a critical legal analysis. An attempt has been made by the present study to address precisely all these issues.

2

Intellectual Property Rights in Life Forms and Farmers

The distribution of property rights over biological resources has been a longstanding concern in international law. Indeed one of the cardinal principles of international law since decolonisation has been the permanent sovereignty of states over their Natural resources.[1] The question of sovereignty has remained extremely sensitive and constitutes, for instance, one important factor explaining the lack of an international legal framework governing the management of forests until today. In recent years, debates over the allocation of biological resources have been intensified at the international level. This is first, due to concerns related to the conservation of biodiversity linked to the ever-increasing exploitation of biological resources on a global level. Second, scientific advances in the field of genetic engineering/biotechnology have opened significant new economic opportunities. In the

1. General Assembly Resolution 1803 (XVII), Permanent Sovereignty Over Natural Resources, 14th December, 1962.

context of economic globalisation this has made the issues of access, use and control over biological resources a topic of increasing interest in international forums. *In recent years, however, the issue of control over the resources themselves has been superseded by questions concerning Bio-diversity-related knowledge and inventions.* Intellectual-property rights concerning biodiversity have thus been in the limelight. The introduction of intellectual property rights has been controversial because nature and nature-related knowledge were, for a long time, excluded from the framework of Intellectual property law.

The right to prevent others from using ideas or information to their own commercial advantage is not easily delineated. Legal technique of some sophistication is called for and this has until recently made intellectual property a somewhat esoteric specialism. A widening circle of people needs some knowledge of what they involve. International negotiations about intellectual property proliferate but legal protection is still at base a matter for the domestic laws of national states. As transnational business grows so does the experts need to have some acquaintance with IPR laws of all major countries and the impact on their constitutional systems.

The utilitarian justification views IPR (patents, trademarks, registered designs, copyrights, etc.) as a means towards encouraging invention and innovation in society.[2] "Economic studies of the patent system often stress the difference between the opportunity cost to the inventor and the opportunity cost to the other developers in bringing an invention to the market place, and conceptualize the invention as a 'public good'. The patent System is seen as a means of evening the distribution of these costs".[3]

Law in the area of life patenting has been developing in the west for the last two decades, keeping pace with the developments in biotechnology. According to Iver P. Cooper[4]

2. B.S. Chimni, *'The Philosophy of Patents : Strong Regime Unjustified'*, Journal for Scientific and Industrial Research. Volume 52, 1993, pp. 234-39.
3. Iver, P. Cooper, *Biotechnology and the Law*, Volume 1, p. 1.1, Pub-West Group.
4. *Ibid.*, p. VII.

"Biotechnology is a new word for an old idea, the idea of a technology based on the use of other living things". The advancements in this area proved that genetic constitution of living beings can be altered. This resulted in the emergence of genetic engineering as a scientific revolution which promises even the creation of new life. The subject matters of biotechnological inventions are micro-organisms, hybrid plants, genetically engineered animals, Gene therapy, genetically engineered vaccines and new anti-body technology, Recombinant DNA technology popularly known as genetic engineering, used for developing disease resistant plants, herbicide resistant crops human genes and cell lines. The high commercial potential of genetic researches made this branch of science a focal point of trade and investment. The new biotechnological approach implies that crops as such are not the raw materials, but rather the compound in them—starch, protein, fats and oils, etc. As such, producers of such commodities, farmers, fishermen and big multinational companies will all be competing with each other for selling their commodities in the international market—a competition between unimaginable unequals.[5]

Consequently claims for patents on those living inventions have started coming up along with a demand for better patent protection for biotechnological inventions. Biotechnology inventions pose a unique problem because any exchange of reproductive material between the developer and other independent parties creates the potential of multiplying the genotype to the detriment of the developer, particularly as it normally requires less expertise to multiply the genotype than to develop it. Thus, the lure of the shadowy world of trade secrets is very great, and only the developer with confidence in the patent system will resist it when trade secret protection is commercially feasible.

This led to a situation where law and legal systems were compelled to address the issue of granting patents on living

5. R.N. Basu, *Biotechnology and Bioethics*, pp. 10-44. Pub. Paschimbanga Bignan Mancha, Kolkata.

beings, particularly in the context of globalisation of trade and investment.

DEVELOPMENT IN US

The US supreme court in Chakraborty[6] case liberally interpreted the patentability norm contained is 35 USC Section 101, and held that a man-made micro-organism is patentable. This was the first patent on a life form. The court, in the case, considered whether a micro-organism constitutes *a manufacture of composition of matters* within the meaning of the statute. The court in 5:4 majority judgment interpreted the above expression as including living subject matter also. The decision created a tempest in the intellectual circles resulting in heated debates about the various ramifications of providing patents on life forms. The debate still goes on.

Subsequent to Chakrabarty case the court in Exparte Allen[7] extended patent protection to multicellular organisms. A few days after the decision in this case the PTO Commissioner in the US issued a statement which reads as follows:

> *The patent and trademark office now consider non-naturally occurring non-human multicellular organisms, including animals to be patentable subject matter within the scope of 35 USC.*[8]

This statement is now reflected as the policy in the manual of patent examining procedure.[9] Based on this policy the US Patent office granted the first patent on an animal the Harvard Oncomouse.[10] The patent was for transgenic non-human mammal. The mouse disclosed in this patent was bearing activated oncogenes in its genome as a result of which

6. Diamond *vs*. Chakrabarty (1980) SC, 447 US 303.
7. 1987 2 U S PQ, 2 d 1425.
8. United States Official Gazette, April 21, 1987.
9. Harward, T. Markey, *'Patentibility of Animals in the US'20 IIC*, 372 (1987), p. 376.
10. US Patent No. 4736866.

it had an increased susceptibility to cancer.[11] Even though this patent is generally referred to as the Harvard Oncomouse patent, the claims allowed under the patent were of considerable breadth and not limited to mice.

After the Harvard oncomouse patent, no patents were issued till 1992 and in December 1992 further patents were granted on transgenic mice. Patenting of living beings in U.S. is no more confined to micro-organisms. In 1995 the scientists at the University of Utah succeeded in finding BRCA, the breast cancer gene. They got it patented in US and the small biotech company which they started, to commercially exploit the invention, turned to be a market giant.[12] Subsequently, W. French Anderson of the national Institute of Health (NIH) of US obtained a broad patent on human gene therapy in 1995. Mammals, human genes and cell lines, nothing is left out now from the purview of patents in US.

DEVELOPMENT IN EUROPE

The European Patent Office (EPO) following closely the US Patent Office practices has granted numerous patents on all sorts of biological materials.[13] Though not explicitly mentioned, it is generally accepted that EPC allows patent protection for micro-organisms.[14] The technical board of Appeal of the

11. Patricia, A. Rac, *'Patentibility of living subject matter'*, 10 CIPR 4 (1993).
12. Malcolm Gladwell, *'Are scientists wrong to patent genes'*—Span, April/May 1996, 54, p. 52.
13. e.g. :
    (i) T 162/86. 'Plasmid PSGZ/HOECHSTAG', OJEPO, 1988, 492.
    (ii) T. 288/86. 'Boving growth hormone. The regents of the University of California'.
    (iii) T. 118/87. 'Anylobytic enzymes/CPC' OJEPO, 1991, 74-479.
    (iv) T. 39/88. 'Micro organisms/CPC' OJEPO, 1989, 499, 502.
14. Article 53 (b) of European patent convention says that the exclusion of plants or animal varieties or essentially biological progresses does not apply to products of microbiological processes.

European Patent Office in a number of cases upheld EPOs decisions in granting patents on plants and seeds.[15]

In Europe too moving away from their earlier stand the European council biotech directive broadens the European patent regime and brings with in its scope a wide range of biological materials. Article 2 of the directive defines the expression biological material in the following lines :

> "Biological material means any material containing genetic information and capable of self-producing or capable of being reproduced in a biological system". According to Article 4(2) of the directive, plants and animals as well as elements of plants and animals are patentable subject matter. The new patentability norms provided in the directive exclude human beings as a whole and human embryos from patentability. The above mentioned march/evolution of law has deeply influenced the patentability norms set under the TRIPS Agreement. The TRIP, under Art 27, mandates for patenting of micro-organism.[16] India being a member of the WTO was required to provide product patents on micro-organism before Jan 1st, 2004,[17] which has already been done vide the patent (Amendment) Act, 2002 as is evidenced by the following amended portion of S3 of the patent Act, 1970 (as amended 2002). In S3 (i) the words "or plants" have been omitted by the patents (Amendment) Act, 2002, S4(d)(ii)—omission from exclusion clause implies inclusion in "invention". Thus, any process for the medicinal, surgical, curative, prophylactic . . . or any process for a similar treatment of animals to render them free of disease or to increase their economic value or that of their products (in the case of plants) is not excluded from patentability and thus patentable.

In S3 (j) added by the patents (Amendment) Act, 2002,

15. Re Ciba-Geigy AG. 749/83. OJEPO, 3/198 4172 (EPO Tech Bd of App).
16. Article 27(1) and 27(3)(b) of the TRIPS Agreement.
17. Article 65(4) of TRIPS.

S4(e) the words, "other than micro-organism" implies exclusion from exclusion clause which in turn implies non exclusion from patentability. Thus "micro-organism" can be "inventions" and thus patentable.

The above mentioned changes in law meet the requirement of TRIPS U/WTO, an obligation which India must discharge within Jan 1st 2004 being a signatory to WTO. India has also already enacted the protection of Plant Varieties and Farmers' Rights Act, 2001 to ensure 'sui generis' law to protect plant Varity, breeders rights, and farmers' rights in response to the TRIPS mandate.

INDIAN JUDICIAL INITIATIVE

Calcutta High Court on 15th January 2002 has given a landmark decision[18] allowing claim for grant of patent to genetically engineered micro-organism called infectious bursitis vaccine.

The appellant had filed a patent application for an inventive process of preparing infectious bursitis vaccine. The application was rejected by the Patent Authorities on the ground that :

1. The process of preparing a vaccine having living entity cannot be considered as manufacture.
2. The above mentioned process is not an invention according to Sec. 2(1) of the Patent Act, 1970.
3. A process to be covered under invention must result in a substance and a vaccine with a living organism cannot be considered as a substance.

Contention of the appellant was that preparation of infectious bursitis vaccine is an invention because :

---

18. Dimminaco A.G. *vs.* Controller of Patents Designs and Trade marks (Unreported—for details of Case See *IPR Bulletin,* Vol. 8, Nos. 7-9. July-September 2002, published by Technology Information, Forecasting and Assessment Council (TIFAC). Department of Science and Technology, New Delhi.

1. The process involves *inventive steps* and the invented vaccine protect poultry against infectious Bursitis.
2. There is no bar in present Indian law against patenting of end product, the manufacture of which involve live virus.
3. The patent claimed in the present case is only for process for preparation of vaccine itself.

Taking into consideration the arguments of both sides. The High Court held as under:

1. Controller erred himself in law by holding that merely because end product contain live virus, process involved is not an invention.
2. The claim of patent should have been considered by Controller on principles of Sec. 3 of the Patent Act. No objection was raised by examiners under Sec. 3.
3. Applying the vendibility test the vaccine was treated as substance.

The Court directed Controller to reconsider the application for grant of patent to appellant. It is submitted that this judgment has opened new opportunities for obtaining patents in India on micro-organism-related inventions which were hitherto not granted.

REACTION TO THE AFOREMENTIONED DEVELOPMENT OF IPR LAWS

The decisions of the European parliament to give green signal to the directive aforementioned attracted criticism from various corners. Environmentalist and NGOs call it a clear demonstration of democratic unaccountability. The various judicial bodies which were called upon to address the issue did not venture to look at it objectively in the light of the moral, ethical and environmental dimension involved in it. The resultant judicial process therefore failed to reflect upon the compelling rational involved in it. This gave rise to the legal recognition of undesirable standards incompatible with larger social needs thereby lacking universal acceptability. This development of the law created world wide uproar among various CSOs, NGOs, jurists, etc. and to counter the initiatives of the biotechnology industry to "monopolise ownership of seed the first link in food chain"[19] through IPR/Patents, the concept of Flamers' Rights emerged. The basic concept was that while a commercial variety could generate returns to the commercial breeder (notably on the basis of Plant Breeders' Rights (PBRs/patents), no system of compensation or incentive for the providers of germplasm had been developed.[20] Genetic resources have been declared to be the common heritage of mankind. This has led to a blatantly unfair situation in which use of these resources has never been paid for. *While countries like Canada and Germany are able to earn from their copper and coal, how could the third world be denied of the opportunity to earn from it's biological diversity? Rice, potato and cotton plants were not lying around in the forests waiting to be picked up. Food and cash crops on which the very survival of human race is based, were created in tropics, from wild plants by generations of careful breeding and selections. This innovative laborious process carried out by the farmers of the third world has gifted the world a stable secure food supply and many grain dollars to countries, exporting agricultural surplus. The third world farmers have not only selected almost all important crops but also have identified in several cases, the genetic traits that gave these crops desirable characteristics. The first disease resistant potatoes were bred by farmers of Bolivia. To the west African farmers goes the credit of breeding some of the first insect resistant bean varieties, rice and certain varieties of wheat were bred by Indian farmers.*[21]

FARMERS' RIGHTS—ORIGIN AND DEVELOPMENT

The origin of the concept of farmers' rights can be traced in the debates held within FAO on the asymmetry in the

19. V. Shiva, *'Agricultural Biodiversity, Intellectual Property Rights and Farmers' Rights'*, Economic and Political Weekly, June 22, 1996, p. 1622.
20. Esquinas Alcazar, 1996, p. 4.
21. Ramaswami and Ballasundaram—*'Impact of GATT on Indian Agricultural Biodiversity and Patenting Issues'*, Productivity, Volume 42, 3 October-December 2001.

distribution of benefits between farmers as donors of germplasm and the producers of commercial varieties that ultimately rely on such germplasm. The basic concept was that while a commercial variety could generate returns to the commercial breeder (notably on the basis of plant Breeders' Rights (PBRs), "no system of compensation or incentives for the providers of germplasm" had been developed.[22] The concept of Farmers' Rights was incorporated in an International Undertaking. This Undertaking (adopted by the FAO Conference in 1983) is a non-binding instrument under which the State parties agreed to provide other parties adhering to the Undertaking[23] "free access" to the plant genetic resources within their territory.[24] The principle of "free access" in this context, however, did not necessarily mean "free of charge", as clarified by Article 5a of Resolution 4/89.

Under these provisions countries could not, in principle, prevent access to plant genetic resources residing in their territories, but they could certainly establish the condition under which such access could take place. This point was later developed by the Convention on Biological Diversity, which made access (although not restricted to non-commercial purposes) conditional upon "mutually agreed terms" and the sharing of benefits obtained as a result of the access.

The establishment of such a system of free access under the International Undertaking provoked some concerns in

22. Esquinas Alcazar, 1996, p. 4.
23. In accordance with article 5b of Resolution 4/89, the benefits to be derived from the Undertaking are "part of a reciprocal system, and should be limited to countries adhering to the International Convention".
24. The Parties Undertook "To allow access to samples of such resources, and to permit their export, where the resources have been requested for the purpose of scientific research, plant breeding or genetic resource conservation. The samples will be made available free of charge, on the basis of mutual exchange or on mutually agreed terms". (Article 5 of the International Undertaking). In addition, in accordance with Resolution 4/89, "A state may impose only such minimum restrictions on the free exchange of materials covered by Article 2.1(a) of the international undertaking as are necessary for it to conform to its national and international obligations" (Article 2 of the Agreed Interpretation).

developed countries regarding the situation of materials under private control, particularly those protected by PBRs. The aim of the International Undertaking was not to prejudge the means of appropriation that countries (while exercising their sovereign rights) could establish in respect of plant genetic resources. Hence, it was recognized that:

> *"Plant Breeders' Rights as provided for under UPOV (international Union for the Protection of New varieties of Plants) are not incompatible with the International Undertaking"* (Article 1 of the Agreed Interpretation, FAO Resolution 4/89).

In recognizing the legitimacy of plant breeders' rights, a serious asymmetry became apparent, for while breeders were able to secure property rights over the varieties they created and the associated benefits, the value-added by traditional farmers (who over time had persistently conserved and improved those materials later on used by breeders) received no recognition at all.

The concept of Farmers' Rights thus emerged as a means to provide a counterbalance to intellectual property rights. It was first introduced by FAO Resolution 4/89, unanimously approved by more than 160 countries, and was further defined by FAO Resolution 5/89 as,

> "Rights arising from the past, present and future contribution of farmers in conserving, improving and making available Plant Genetic Resources, particularly those in the centers of original diversity. These rights are vested in the International Community, as trustees for present and future generations of farmers, for the purpose of ensuring full benefits of farmers and supporting the continuation of their contributions."

One of the objectives of Farmers' Rights, in accordance with the same Resolution, is to allow farmers, their communities and countries in all regions, fully to participate in the benefits derived, at present and in the future, from the improved use of Plant Genetic Resources through plant breeding and other scientific methods.

In sum, the concept of Farmers' Rights was adopted with a view to realizing the objective of balancing the rights of traditional breeders and of plant breeders, while allowing the farmers to benefit, in some way, from the value that they have creatively contributed. Though the concept was only defined in a broad, imprecise manner, it recognized the role of farmers as custodians of biodiversity and helped to call attention to the need to preserve practices that are essential for a sustainable agriculture. The adoption of that concept fostered an intense debate on the ways to recognize and reward traditional farmers, not only to the current benefit of such farmers but in order to ensure the community of activities that are crucial for humanity at large.

Since the adoption of the concept of Farmers' Rights, considerable empirical evidence has highlighted the role of traditional farmers in relation to plant genetic resources.[25] The idea of recognizing Farmers' Rights transcended FAO and the International Undertaking and was also supported in other international fora. This concept was reaffirmed in various contexts, namely:

- Chapter 14.60(a) of Agenda 21 (approved at the UN Conference on Environment and Development held in Rio de Janeiro in 1992), stated that the appropriate United Nations agencies and regional organizations should "strengthen the Global System on the Conservation and Sustainable Use of Plant Genetic Resources For Food and Agriculture (PGRFA) by taking further steps to realize Farmers' Rights".
- Resolution 3 of the Nairobi Conference for the Adoption of an Agreed Text of the Convention on Biological Diversity, identified the realization of Farmers' Rights as one of the "outstanding issues" for further negotiation.

25. For example, Glachant and Leveque, 1993; Louvaars and Marrewijk, 1996; Evension, Gollin and Santaniello (Editors), 1998; Brush (Ed.), 2000.

- The Global Plan of Action for the Conservation and sustainable Utilization of Plant Genetic Resources for Food and Agriculture, included the realization of Farmers' Rights at the national, regional and international level, as one of the long-term objectives of the Plan, in the context of *in situ* conservation.[26]
- A June 1999 study by the Economic and Social Council (ECOSOC) on the Right to Food, submitted to the Commission on Human Rights, urged that Farmers' Rights be promoted as part of the "Right to Food", especially since "our future food supply and its sustainability may depend on such rights being established on a firm footing" (Commission on Human Rights, 1999).
- The convention on Biological Diversity (CBD) did not explicitly address the issue of Farmers' Rights. Nevertheless, according to article 8 of the CBD, each Contracting Party shall "as far as possible and as appropriate",

  ". . . subject to its national legislation, respect, preserve and maintain knowledge, innovations and practices of indigenous and local communities embodying traditional lifestyles relevant for the conservation and sustainable use of biological diversity and promote their wider application with the approval and involvement of the holders of such knowledge, innovations and practices and encourage the equitable sharing of the benefits arising from the utilization of such knowledge, innovations and practices. . . "

This provision is programmatic in nature and requires to be implemented by the Contracting Parties through specific measures to be adopted at the national level. A Conference of

26. However, no firm and clear commitments were made at the Leipzig Conference (which adopted the Global plan) with regard to the form of implementation of such rights, Berhan and Egzibher 1996.

these Parties had been convened to consider this issue,[27] but little progress has been made so far on the concrete ways to provide protection to traditional knowledge.[28] Despite lack of a specific reference to the concept of Farmers' Rights, the CBD may be considered a relevant framework for the implementation of some components of such Rights particularly with regard to the sharing of benefits and for funding (Articles 15.7 and 20). These benefits include access to, and transfer of, technology, which makes use of the genetic resources provided (Article 16.3); participation in biotechnological research using such genetic resources (Article 19.1); and priority access to the results and benefits arising from such biotechnological research (Article 19.2) (FAO, 1994a, Para 8).

Some proposal for national legislation have also reaffirmed the concept of Farmers' Rights. An example of the possible implementation of such Rights at the national level is offered by the law on plant varieties protection in India.[29] Farmers' Rights are not specifically defined.[30]

However, Sec. 39 of The Protection of Plant Varieties and Farmers' Rights Act, 2001 states that :

27. For example, document UNPEP/CBD/COP/3/L.13, 13 November 1996. The parties agreed to establish an *ad hoc* open-ended inter-sessional working group to address the implementation of Article 8(j) and related provisions to be composed of Parties and observers including, in particular, representatives of indigenous peoples and local communities. The Working Group held its first Meeting in Seville, in March 2000.
28. WIPO has also initiated studies on the matter, in the context of its "Program on Global Intellectual Property Issues". See The Crucible II Group, 2000, pp. 72-85.
29. The Protection of Plants Varieties and Farmers' Rights Act, 2001.
30. An earlier version of the bill defined Farmers' Rights as Follows : "The Farmers' Rights for the purpose of this Act mean the rights arising from the past, present and expected future contributions of farmers in ensuring conservation, improvement and availability of plant genetic resources, particularly in the centers of origin or diversity through a continuous engagement in an on-farm evolution of variations within varieties. For their above said contributions, the farmers are entitled to full benefits and support in the condition of their contribution" (Section 22.ii).

Sec. 39. Farmers' Right.—(1) Notwithstanding anything contained in this Act—

(i) a farmer who has bred or developed a new variety shall be entitled for registration and other protection in like manner as a breeder of a variety under this Act;

(ii) the farmers' variety shall be entitled for registration if the application contains declaration as specified in clause (h) of sub-section (1) of section 18;

(iii) a farmer who is engaged in the conservation of genetic resources of land races and wild relatives of economic plants and their improvement through selection and preservation shall be entitled in the prescribed manner for recognition and reward from the Gene Fund;
Provided that material so selected and preserved has been used as donors of genes in varieties registrable under this act; and

(iv) a farmer shall be deemed to be entitled to save, use, sow, resow, exchange, share or sell his farm produce including seed of a variety protected under this Act in the same manner as he was entitled before the coming into force of this Act :
Provided that the farmer shall not be entitled to sell branded seed of a variety protected under this Act.

Explanation—For the purposes of clause (iv), "branded seed" means any seed put in a package or any other container and labeled in a manner indicating that such seed is of a variety protected under this Act.

(2) Where any propagating material of a variety registered under this Act has been sold to a farmer or a group of farmers or any organization of farmers, the breeder of such variety shall disclose to the farmer or the group of farmers or the organization of farmers, as the case may be, the expected performance under given conditions, and if such propagating material fails to provide such performance under such given conditions, the farmer or the group of farmers or the organization of farmers, as the case may be, may claim

compensation in the prescribed manner before the Authority and the Authority shall after giving notice to the breeder of the variety and after providing him an opportunity to file opposition in the prescribed manner and after hearing the parties, it may direct the breeder of the variety to pay such compensation as it deems fit, to the farmer or the group of farmers or the organization of farmers, as the case may be.[31]

Another interesting feature of the law is the establishment of a system of "benefit-sharing" based on "the extent and nature of the use of genetic materials" of the claimant in the development of the protected variety, and on the commercial value and demand in the market. The determined amount of benefit-sharing should be deposited by the breeder in a "National Gene Fund" (S45);[32] which would also receive "a fee by way of royalty" to be paid annually by every breeder that the Central Government may impose for the retention of the registration under the Act. The Fund would cover, among other things, "the expenditure for supporting the conservation and sustainable use of genetic resources including *in situ* and *ex situ* collections". [S45 (2) (C)]

Other proposals for the recognition of the rights of local, indigenous and farmers' communities at the national level include the following[33] :

- An "African Model Legislation for the Recognition and protection of the Rights of Local Communities,

31. This text replaces a provision contained in previous drafts, according to which "Nothing shall affect the farmers' traditional rights to save, use, exchange, share and sell his farm produce of the protected variety except sale for reproductive purpose under commercial marketing arrangements" (Section 17).
32. According to an earlier version of the law, the funds of a "National Community Gene Fund" would be utilized in trust for Indian farmers for collecting, evaluating, upgrading, conserving and utilizing genetic variability. One of the resources of the Fund would have been based on a percentage of the total sales of protected varieties. The law would have implemented through this mechanism, the sharing of benefits in the gains accruing from the commercial exploitation of germplasm (Srinivasan, 1996, p. 81).
33. The Crucible II Group, 2000, pp. 96-97.

Farmers and Breeders and for the Regulation of Access of Genetic Resources" was developed by the Organization of African Unity's (OAU). Part V of the draft defines the concept and the scope of Farmers' Rights.

- The Zambian Government has drafted a plant variety protection law that seeks to protect the innovations of local communities and indigenous peoples in keeping with its obligations under the CBD.
- In Thailand, a draft Plant Variety Protection Bill would combine recognition for the rights of plant breeders to their newly developed varieties with the protection of native varieties that have been conserved and developed by farmers and local communities.
- The Plant Varieties Act of Bangladesh, drafted by the National Committee on Plant Genetic Resources, recognizes community rights and Farmers' Rights, and proposes the establishment of a fund to support communities in the conservation and development of plant varieties.
- Costa Rica's "Biodiversity Law" (May 1998) recognize and expressly protects the practices and innovations of indigenous peoples and local communities related to the use of biodiversity components and their associated knowledge. The law obliges the competent authority to reject any request for recognition of intellectual or industrial rights for biodiversity components or knowledge that is already recognized by community rights.

In sum, the concept of Farmers' Rights has been recognized in various international instruments, including as a component of Human Rights. It also finds support in the CBD in the context of article 8(j), while it has also begun to receive recognition in national legislation.

JURISPRUDENTIAL RATIONALE OF FARMERS' RIGHTS

Though there has been little academic work on the concept of Farmers' Rights,[34] the debate that took place within FAO and in other fora has helped to clarify the rationale for the recognition of such Rights. Such rationale seems to be grounded on three sets of considerations, relating to equity, the need to ensure the conservation of plant genetic resources for food and agriculture, and the establishment of barriers to conventional IPRs that may restrict farmers' practices with respect to saving, selling and exchanging seeds. These considerations are briefly examined below.

1. Equity

Conservation (*in situ*, including on farm, and *ex situ*), research and development, and the utilization of plant genetic resources, are components of a complex system in dynamic interaction. Such an interaction is based on market and non-market relationships among different types of agents with specific functions within a system that may be called the "Plant Genetic Resources System".[35] Agents in the plant genetic resources system include traditional farmers and indigenous communities, collectors and curators (conservation subsystem), research institutions (research and development subsystem) breeders and seed companies (commercial breeding/ production subsystem), and farmers (agricultural use subsystem).

Each of these groups perform different functions within a particular framework of customary and legal rules. The dividing lines between these activities are not, however, always clear-cut. Thus, traditional farmers undertake empirical research at the farm level not just on varieties but also on cultivation techniques.

Traditional farmers both conserve and use plant genetic resources (PGR). The value of plant genetic resources is

34. Girsberger, 1999.
35. The following characterization of this system is substantially based on Correa, 2000.

preserved and enhanced by their utilization for planting, seed production and continuous selection of the best adapted farmers' varieties (landraces). Such farmers generally interact among themselves on the basis of barter or exchange across the fence. Thus fostering the diffusion of their varieties and further development.

Collectors and curators collect and/or conserve and manage plant genetic resources, specially with regard to their characterization, cataloguing, evaluation and pre-development. They interact with traditional farmers, research institutions, breeders and seed companies. In most cases, such an interaction is based on non-market transactions. Traditional farmers are not paid for the value they deliver, breeders and seed companies are not charged a price for the samples they obtain. Research institutions utilize plant genetic resources to undertake basic and applied research, including agro-biotechnology, and to enhance existing varieties and the availability of gene-pools. *Interaction with other agents in the system (traditional farmers, curators, breeders) is generally on a non-market basis. However, a strong trend towards protection of research results and increased linkages with private companies is introducing market-based means of interaction.*

Breeders utilize plant genetic resources in breeding programmes. They obtain materials and scientific information from the farmer groups, generally on a non-market basis, and produce new or improved varieties for sale in the market. Intellectual property rights, wherever available, strengthen their market position and their ability to recover development expenditures. Seed companies utilize "breeding" results to propagate and sell seeds. They operate entirely within the market. Plant genetic resources are one of the (intangible) inputs in seed production, though such resources are not attributed a particular value, except where protected by intellectual property rights.

Finally, farmers who utilize improved varieties are at the end of the research/production chain. They benefit from the work undertaken, whether remunerated or not, within other subsystems. Their relationship with seed suppliers is market-based. Farmers both use and produce seeds, which they can reuse freely or in the framework of the "farmers' privilege",[36] where applicable.

While, in sum, traditional farmers create economic value, the problem is that such value has no direct expression through market mechanisms. Some fragmented evidence on the economic benefits obtained by recipients of plant genetic resources is available and provides useful insights on their value.[37] However, the economic value of diversity conserved by traditional farmers for agriculture is difficult to assess.[38]

The value of farmers' varieties is not directly dependent on their current use in conventional breeding, since the gene flow from landraces to privately marketed cultivators of major crops is very modest[39]. Conventional breeding increasingly focuses on crosses among elite materials from the breeders' own collections and advanced lines developed in public institutions. According to one study, material from *ex-situ gene* banks contributed three per cent of the germplasm used by breeders and materials from *in situ* conservation areas a further one per cent.[40]

Though it is expected that the demand for primitive materials may increase in the future,[41] it would be unrealistic to think that substantial value may be derived from current gene flows of landraces held in situ conditions.[42] As a result, any economic measure directly linked to such flows would grossly underestimate the global values generated by farmers' varieties over time. Farmers' rights thus need to be considered, not only on the basis of the added value that they may generate today, but also retroactively address farmers' past contributions.[43]

---

36. This is an exception generally allowed under PBR regimes, which permits farmers to reuse, in their own exploitation, the seeds obtained from the utilization of protected varieties.
37. National Research Council, 1993; Evenson, Gollin, Santaniello, 1998.
38. Brush, 1994.
39. Wright, 1998, p. 229.
40. Swanson and Luxmoore, 1996.
41. Ten Kate, Kerry and Laird, 1999, p. 141.
42. Gollin, 1998, pp. 236-38.
43. Wright, 1998, p. 229.

In sum, traditional farmers create economic value for others, but cannot themselves benefit from it. There is no market for the value they create, however, other agents in the "Plant Genetic Resource System" do benefit from the materials provided by traditional farmers, and obtain specific rights over the germplasm that incorporates what traditional farmers have developed in the past 44.

The development of the concept of Farmers' Rights may be regarded, in this context, as the result of equity considerations: there is a moral obligation to ensure that traditional farmers receive a fair share of the benefits arising from the use of plant genetic resources that they conserve and improve.

2. Conservation

A second element underlying the rationale of Farmers' Rights relate to their possible role as an instrument to support the conservation of plant genetic resources for food and agriculture.

Maintenance of biological diversity in farming systems generates value for the global community which is determined by the following components:

1. A "portfolio effect", namely, the static value of retaining a wide range of varieties and methods of production, which reduces the risk of variability of production;
2. A "quasi option value", based on the value of the future flow of expected information to be generated by the retained diversity; and
3. An "exploration value", or the value of retaining the evolutionary process of varieties and the opportunity of discovering new traits and characteristics.[45]

Farmers benefit from the availability of germplasm to face changes in the environment, diseases or pests ("quasi-option" value). The "exploration value" may be of particular

44. FAO, 1994a, para. 41.
45. Swanson, Pearce and Cervigni, 1994, p. 26.

importance for biotechnology-based industries, which can exploit genes of particular agronomic interest. Consumers, finally, benefit from a reduced risk of variability in production ("portfolio value") and from better and more production. These values can not be appropriated by farmers, in the absence of a market mechanism or other specific instruments that put an obligation to pay on those receiving the benefits.

The economic value of plant genetic resources may also be analysed, in marginal terms, on the basis of the opportunity cost of the conversion of biodiversity to specialized production. While conserving landraces, traditional farmers are deprived of obtaining higher productivity and income associated with the use of modern varieties. There is, therefore, a value determined by the differential in the average yield between the use of land in a traditional as opposed to a specialized form the production.[46]

Farmers holding landraces, thus create an economic value but they are currently unable to appropriate it for the purposes of generating an income. There is a market failure that undervalues, or does not value at all farmers' contributions. In economic terms, farmers generate externalities as providers of a "global public good".[47] The direct beneficiaries of the value created by the non-conversion of land from traditional to specialized use are those who are able to utilize downstream the germplasm so conserved. The existence of greater diversity also has a significant positive impact on the stability of food supply.

Farmers' Rights may be seen, in this context, as a means of ensuring that plant genetic resources for food and agriculture are conserved and continue to be made available.[48] However, the implementation of such rights should not be

46. *Ibid.*, p. 25.
47. The beneficiaries of the value created by traditional farmers include breeders and farmers of all countries, and not only of the country where the relevant landrace was developed, for in most cases those resources are found in several countries. Their distribution is not constrained by national boundaries (Fowler, 2000).
48. (FAO, 1994a, para-41) : This instrumental approach clearly excludes a concept of Farmers' Rights based solely on farmers' interests.

regarded as a means of rendering the conservation conditioned on such rights but as a general support to the traditional farmers' activities.[49] In other words, it may be difficult too hold that, in the absence of a prompt realization of Farmers' Rights, the traditional farmers will abruptly cease in their role as conservers of plant diversity, or that the intensity of such activities will be directly dependent, at least in the short-term, on such realization.[50] But it may be affirmed that some part of farmers' biodiversity is lost every day and if no action is taken, in the long-term such activities will be substantially weakened, putting at risk the survival of an essential component of the Plant Genetic Resources System.

This point may be illustrated by way of a comparison with IPRs. The conventional theory argues that in the absence of IRPs, there will be an inadequate investment in research and development, since there will be no means to ensure the recovery of expenditures made. Thus, IRPs are regarded as a condition for an optimal investment in such activities, in contrast, the realization of Farmers' Rights, conceived as a non-exclusive mechanism, cannot be reasonably assumed to be indispensable for the continuation of conservation activities that are taking place as an integral part of existing agricultural system in a large number of countries. These systems are not dependent, like IPRs, on the creation of extraordinary rents through exclusive market positions but, to the contrary, on an open system of exchange and circulation of materials.

In sum, the concept of Farmers' Rights may be justified as a useful tool to support conservation activities undertaken by traditional farmers. The realization of such Rights would aim to ensure the continuation of such activities, to the benefit of present and future generations.

3. Preservation of Farmers' Practices

A third element underlying the concept of Farmers' Rights is the need to provide a counterbalance to conventional

49. Esquinas Alcazar, 1996, p. 15.
50. This fact may help to explain why to date there has been no sense of "urgency" in the negotiation of a revised International Undertaking, and with regard to the realization of Farmers' Rights. See Petit *et al.*, 2000.

intellectual property rights such as patents and PBRs, and thereby to avoid the creation of barriers against the farmers' use and improvement of plant genetic resources. The basic issue here is that the conservation and continuous development of farmers' variety is dependent upon the possibility of saving and exchanging seeds, particularly within their communities.

Seed supply systems may be broadly grouped in three categories :

1. The "informal" system characterized by farmers engaged in seed-saving, in bartering with neighbours or farmers in different villages and purchasing seeds from local grain stalls;
2. A "transitional" system in which some farmers specialize in the production of seeds for the local market; and
3. The "commercial" system where the seeds are provided by private companies and/or public and semi-public institutions.

The "informal" system is based on the use and continuous improvement of farmers' varieties. It operates on the basis of the diffusion of the best seeds available within a community, and on their movement, even over large distances "during migration or after disaster. . . In these systems genetic material is valued highly, for example, as a gift, but it does not represent a monetary value (because it can be reproduced). It is unlikely that the spread of varieties has ever been restricted out of ownership considerations".[51]

The "commercial" system requires strict control over various cycles of production of genetic, physiological, physical and sanitary parameters. Considerable time and investment is devoted to obtaining "uniform" varieties, which normally requires the planting of a few generations before homogeneity can be described and claimed. Though the conventional breeding method is widely available, mature technology, the necessary investments and the time required for releasing new

51. Louwaars, 1996, p. 1-1.

varieties, all constitute considerable barriers of entry, and are the basis of the demands for IPRs protection or other mechanisms that protect and reward such investments.

The diffusion of commercial varieties has generally evolved through different stages. It usually begins with improved varieties developed or adopted from plant breeding, focusing on major crops in favourable areas. During the second stage, a wider range of varieties and hybrids are developed and commercialized, farmers' varieties being replaced with commercial seed. In a final stage, all or most seeds are developed and traded by specialized suppliers, mainly in the private sector.

Thus in developed countries seed is chiefly supplied commercially, mainly by the private sector, even if public institutions actively participate in the development of plant varieties. In developing countries, the informal system is the main channel for diffusing improved varieties; more than 80 percent of crops cultivated in such countries are planted with seeds from the informal seed system.

In most developing countries, however, the commercial and informal systems coexist to a different extent, often in association with a transitional system of seed supply. Thus, in many such countries the commercial production and distribution of seeds is a marginal activity while the informal seed system is dominant. In Ethiopia, for instant, only 2 percent of seed used by small farmers is commercially supplied, while overall, commercial seed constitutes only 5 per cent of the total seeds used. Newly established commercial systems in developing countries are seldom expected to supply more than 15 per cent of total seeds requirements for the specified crops.[52]

The functioning of each seed supply system is dependent on a number of specific factors. Thus, the development of commercial seed sector crucially depends on the existence of an adequate research infrastructure and distribution systems. Commercial breeders' income may be maximized when farmers are unable to save seed and reproduce a variety due

52. Srivastava and Jaffee, 1993, pp. 7-8.

to characteristics of the seeds (such as in the case of hybrids), or due to the local conditions (e.g. germination due to poor storage conditions) that do not provide the maintenance of minimum quality levels.[53] The effective application of IPRs is generally regarded, as mentioned above, as an important element for encouraging investments in research and breeding.[54]

In the case of informal system, farmers' practices of saving and exchanging seeds are essential for preserving the dynamics of the system. If such practices were restricted by IPRs or other barriers, the possibility of continuously improving farm varieties would be blocked, and the system as such may collapse. This is the reason why many views have been expressed stressing the need for defining Farmers' Rights to reflect the inalienable right of every farmer and farming community to save and exchange seed.[55]

In sum, given the coexistence of different systems of seed supply and the impact that IPRs may have on the preservation of the informal system, the recognition of Farmers' Rights can be justified as a means to neutralize possible IPRs-based restrictions on farmers' practices relating to planting back and exchanging seeds.

FARMERS' RIGHTS VS. INTELLECTUAL PROPERTY RIGHTS (IPRs)

1. Relationship

The recognition of "Farmers' Rights", as mentioned in earlier sections, is one of the possible ways to compensate traditional farmers for their contributions to agriculture. Though the content and scope of Farmers' Rights has not been yet fully defined, an important question is whether they can in some way be assimilated to or become, a new form of IPRs.

53. Louwaars, 1996, p. 1-1.
54. See, however, Venner and Alston found that PBRs in the USA did not result in increasing commercial or experimental yields of wheat, but rather served as a "marketing tool" (Venner & Alston, 1999, p. 17).
55. The Crucible II Group, 2000, p. 99.

Different views and options have been suggested on the relationship between these two categories of rights, including.[56]

1. There should be no relationship between Farmers' Rights and IPRs.
2. Farmers' Rights could be recognized in laws relating to plant breeders' rights.[57]
3. A *sui generis* regime on Farmers' Rights should be established separately from existing forms of IPRs.
4. The existing definitions under plant breeders' legislation should be extended to protect farmers' varieties.[58]

In any case, the prevailing opinion is that the recognition of Farmers' Rights would not be incompatible with the obligations of WTO Member countries under the TRIPs Agreement,[59] or with the International Union for the Protection of New Varieties of Plant (UPOV) Convention[60] (The rationale for Farmers' Rights, as presented above, significantly differs from that for patents, copyrights and plant breeders' rights. Farmers' Rights "may not be in themselves, strictly speaking, an Intellectual Property Rights mechanism"[61], though they may be regarded as providing some counterbalance to "formal" IPRs, since the latter "compensate only for the latest innovation, without acknowledging that, in many cases, these spread out over many human generations, in different parts of the world".[62]

In modern economic theory the recognition of IPRs is grounded on the need to provide an incentive and reward for investments in inventive and creative activities. The granting

56. See Mooney, 1996, pp. 41-42.
57. This approach has been proposed in some draft national laws on PBRS as discussed earlier.
58. See Leskien and Flinter, 1997.
59. Otten, 1996, p. 49.
60. Greengrass, 1996, p. 56.
61. Esquinas Alcazar 1996, p. 15.
62. *Ibid.*, p. 4.

of exclusive rights,[63] which is absent in the case of Farmers' Rights, is deemed necessary to compensate the title-holders for the risk and expenses involved in the inventive/creative process.[64]

There are important differences between Farmers' Rights and IPRs. Such differences are fundamental, which go beyond the type of rights conferred, as summarized in Table 2.1.

Table 2.1
Farmers' Rights *vs.* IPRs

	Farmers' Rights	*IPRs*
Rights Conferred	Compensation, Benefit-sharing	Exclusive rights
Titleholder	Farmer communities, States (?)	Physical, juridical persons
Subject matter	Not precisely defined	Inventions, creative works, plant varieties, signs, designs, etc.
Duration	Unlimited	Limited

Table 2.1 indicates that there are major differences between the two compared concepts, not only in terms of rights granted but, more basically, in relation to the titleholders (possibly farmer communities or the States, in the case of Farmers' Rights) and duration. Most importantly, Farmers' Rights are grounded on the contributions made by farmers over the years in plant breeding and conservation, but they are not restricted to or exercised over a particular subject matter. In contrast, IPRs can only be exercised in relation to subject matter which is defined as precisely as possible.

Some expressions of opinion have emphasized that Farmers' Rights should be linked to certain subject matter. Thus, according to the Rural Advancement Foundation International (RAFI), "Farmers' Rights encompass all aspects of

63. The recognition of a jus excluendi is one of the characteristic elements of IPRs (except for trade secrets).
64. Guttermen, 1997.

plant genetic resources including Germplasm, Information, Funds, Technologies and Systems (GIFTS) that are necessary to make any raw material a usable resource". The GIFTS would be ensured through a consistent international funding mechanism. In RAFI's view, nevertheless, funds would not be used to compensate individual farmers or indigenous people, but to reward meritorious work that encourages conservation and use primarily in developing countries.[65]

2. Farmers' Rights as IPRs?

In accordance with a number of proposals, Farmers' Rights could be realized under an IPRs-type of mechanism. Under this approach, IPRs are regarded as an ethical imperative in recognition of the intellectual contributions of farmers, or as a tool useful to preserve biodiversity and prevent further erosion thereof. Within this line of thought, two main trends may be identified.

On the one hand, there are many proposals to extend the application of current modalities of intellectual property rights, or to amend existing laws and practices, in order to protect certain components of indigenous/traditional knowledge, including farmers' varieties. Such proposals include the following relevant considerations:

1. The application of geographical indications, copyright (protection of folklore) or other intellectual property rights.[66]
2. Increasing the flexibility of the requirements for the protection of traditional plant varieties, by applying, for example, a broader concept of uniformity than that which is generally accepted under UPOV-like plant breeders' rights.[67]
3. Introducing new requirements into existing laws, such as the obligation to declare in a patent

65. RAFI, 1994, p. 35.
66. Correa, 1994.
67. Leskein and Flinter, 1997.

application the origin of materials used to develop the invention so as to facilitate benefit sharing.[68]

Other proposals consider that the existing modalities of IPRs are inadequate to protect such knowledge, and call for the development of new forms of IPRs. A number of variants have been elaborated under this approach, which differ considerably with regard to objectives, scope and possible forms of implementation. In general, the aim of such proposals is the establishment of a comprehensive sui generis regime for indigenous and traditional communities' knowledge, covering knowledge on, inter-alia, medicinal plants, materials useful for agriculture and cultivation practices.[69]

It has also been held that Farmers' Rights should compensate for the use of (1) traditional PGRFA and their wild weed-like relatives, and (2) where appropriate, the related know-how of informal plant breeders, and that they should also act as incentives for *in situ* and *ex situ* conservation and sustainable use of traditional PGRFA, their wild and weed-like relatives, and the related know-how. Farmers' Rights should also balance inadequacies and deficiencies of existing forms of intellectual property rights regarding the protection of these traditional plant varieties and related know-how. According to this view, "as a new form of legal claims, Farmers' Rights complement existing forms of intellectual property rights. They are not, however, intended to compete with, or replace, existing intellectual property rights".[70]

Some authors have argued that in order to realize Farmers' Rights, they should be institutionalized as a form of IPRs. According to Greegrass, for instance, if Farmers' Rights were not conceived as IPRs, it would be "impossible to envisage how such a system could be enforced in practice".[71]

Some developing countries have raised the issue of protection of indigenous and local peoples' rights over their

68. Correa, 1999, p. 20, Non-compliance with such an Obligation May Lead to the Invalidation of the Patent Granted. See, for Example, Decision 390 of the Andean Group.
69. Dutfield, 1999.
70. Girsberger, 1999, p. 205.
71. Greengrass, 1996, p. 56.

collective knowledge in the context of a possible revision of Article 27.3(b) of the TRIPs Agreement.[72] Thus, Kenya, on behalf of the African Group, in preparation for the 1999 WTO ministerial conference submitted a proposal requiring that any *sui generis* law for plant variety protection should provide for the protection of the innovations of indigenous and local farming communities in developing countries, consistent with the Convention on Biological Diversity and the International Undertaking on Plant Genetic Resources. In addition, Peru, Bolivia, Colombia, Ecuador and Nicaragua requested the WTO to study and make recommendations on the most appropriate means of recognizing and protecting traditional knowledge, and to develop a multilateral legal framework "that will grant effective protection to the expressions and manifestations of traditional knowledge".

Proposals made by some developing countries in relation to the review of Article 27.3(b), as well as the positions of some regional groups are summarized in Table 2.2.

The attempts to extending IPRs regimes to farmers' varieties (landraces) and the wild and weedy relatives of crops face serious conceptual and operational difficulties, since the value of such resources lies precisely in their *variability* and their continuing evolution (lack of stability over generations), which makes recognition and tracing very speculative.[73] In addition, if specific genetic traits were used to define the subject matter, it would be extremely difficult to identify the geographical area of origin, since they may occur *in situ* in more than one country, and be found in *ex situ* collections in or out side the country.[74]

Those who question a possible assimilation of Farmers' Rights to IPRs fear that an IPRs form of protection may

72. Article 27.3(b)—which requires the protection of plant varieties under patents, an effective sui generies regime or a combination of both-is subject to an early review, which should have begun in 1999. No agreement has yet emerged in the Council of TRIPs about the objectives and scope of such a review.
73. The lack of stability of farmers' varieties would impose limitations on identifying landraces in a manner suitable for the enforcement of any system that is created (Greengrass, 1996, p. 51).
74. FAO, 1994b, Para. 38.

Table 2.2
Developing Countries' Proposals for the Review of Article 27.3(b) of the TRIPs Agreement

Countries/ Organizations	*Patenting (life forms & biological process)*	*Sui-generis (plant varieties)*
(1)	*(2)*	*(3)*
Kenya[1]	Need five-year extension of transition period Harmonize TRIPs with CBD	Need five year extension of transition period Increase scope of 27.3(b) to include protection of indigenous knowledge and Farmers' Rights Harmonise TRIPs with CBD.
Venezuela[2]	In 2000, introduce mandatory system of IPR protection for traditional knowledge of indigenous and local communities, based on the need to recognize collective rights.	
African Group[5]	Review should be extended + additional five year transition hereafter Review should clarify that plants, animals, micro-organisms, their parts and natural processes cannot be patented.	Review should be extended + additional five year transition after that *Sui-generis* laws should allow for protection of community rights, continuation of farm practices and prevention of anti-competitive practices which threaten food sovereignty Harmonise TRIPs with CBD and IU of FAO.
LDC Group[4]	There should be a formal clarification that naturally occurring plants and animals, as well as their parts (gene sequences), plus essentially	*Sui-generis* provisions must be flexible enough to suit each country's seed supply system Need for extended transition period.

(*Contd.*)

TABLE 2.2 (Contd.)

(1)	(2)	(3)
	biological processes, are not patentable. Incorporate provision that patents must not be granted without prior informed consent of country of origin Patents inconsistent with CBD Art. 15 (access) should not be granted Need for extended transition period.	
Jamica, Sri Lanka, Tanzania, Uganda, Zambia[5]	No patenting of plants without prior informed consent of government and communities in country of origin.	
SAARC[6]	There is a need to prevent piracy of traditional knowledge built around bio-diversity and to seek the harmonization of the TRIPs Agreement with the U.N. Convention on Biological Diversity so as to ensure appropriate returns to traditional communities.	
SADC[7]	The traditional period for implementation of 27.3(b) should be extended and the 2000 review should be delayed. The review of 27.3(b) should harmonize TRIPs with CBD. The exclusion of essentially biological processes from patentability should extended to microbiological processes.	The transitional period for implementation of 27.3(b) should be extended and the 2000 review should be delayed. The review of 27.3(b) should retain the *sui generis* option.
Group of 77[8]	Future negotiations must make operational the provisions relating to the transfer of technology, to the mutual advantage of producers and users of technological knowledge and seek mechanisms for a balanced protection of biological resources and disciplines to protect traditional knowledge.	

Bolivia, Colombia, Ecuador, Nicaragua and Peru[9]	The Seattle Ministerial Conference should adopt a mandate to (a) carry out studies in order to make recommendations on the most appropriate means of recognizing and protecting traditional knowledge (TK) as the subject matter of IPR; (b) initiate negotiations with a view to establishing a multilateral legal framework that will grant effective protection to the expressions and manifestations of TK; (c) complete the legal framework envisaged in paragraph (b) above in time for it to be included as part of the results of the new round of trade negotiations.

Source : GRAIN, 2000.

1. WT/GC/W/23 of 5 July 1999.
2. WT/GC/W/282 of 6 August 1999.
3. WT/GC/W/302 of 6 August 1999.
4. WT/GC/W/251 of 13 July 1999.
5. http://www.foe.org/international/wto/govt.htmlof 2sep.1999.
6. South Asia Association for Regional Cooperation (SAARC), WT/L/326 of 22 October 1999.
7. Southern Africa Development Cooperation (SADC), WT/L/317 of 1 October 1999.
8. WT/MIN(99)/3 of 2 November 1999.
9. WT/GC/W/362 of 12 October 1999.

undermine the free sharing of knowledge and resources among local communities and the world community; furthermore, IPRs could be incompatible with the collective nature of innovation at the community level.[75] In sum, Farmers' Rights may be deemed to counterbalance IPRs but do not share the basic features of the latter, particularly the granting of exclusive rights. As discussed below (chapter 5), *one of the components* of Farmers' Rights could be protection of traditional knowledge relating to farmers' varieties.

75. Berhan and Egziabher, 1996.

3

Plant Variety Protection and Legislation

1. THE INDIAN RESPONSE TO INTERNATIONAL LEGAL DEVELOPMENTS

This chapter explores how proprietary claims to plant genetic resources (PGRs) are asserted and constructed in drafting India's Protection of Plant Varieties and Farmers' Rights Act, 2001, and other laws. These claims have assumed significance, particularly during the past two decades, at global, national and local levels.

The protection of plant varieties by means of intellectual property rights has been a subject of increasing importance in the aftermath of the adoption of the Agreement on Trade-Related Aspects of Intellectual Property Rights (TRIPs).[1] Plant variety protection in TRIPs is premised on the need to provide incentives to private sector actors to engage in plant breeding. The ultimate rationale for plant variety protection is the

1. Agreement on Trade-Related Aspects of Intellectual Property Rights, Marrakesh, 15 Apr. 1994.

enhancement of food security through the provision of new improved varieties and improved availability of seeds through private sector channels.

The introduction of plant variety protection in India has significant implications since seed has traditionally been supplied overwhelmingly by farmers themselves and by the public sector, with the private sector playing a marginal role until recently in most crops. From a legal perspective, the protection of plant varieties remains an issue which is far from settled even though the Protection of Plant Varieties and Farmers' Rights Act was adopted in 2001 in compliance with TRIPs obligations. This is due to a number of reasons: Firstly, plant variety protection is an issue which goes beyond giving incentives to the private sector. In fact, while the TRIPs agreement is the direct trigger for the introduction of plant variety protection, it is not the only relevant treaty. The Biodiversity Convention and the International Treaty on Plant Genetic Resources for Food and Agriculture (PGRFA Treaty) are also of major importance.[2] Secondly, while plant variety protection is directly related to innovation in the field of agriculture, it must also be understood in the broader context which includes conservation of biological resources. Thirdly, plant variety protection is opposed to the idea that agricultural management should be based on the sharing of knowledge and resources. This may be criticized from a conceptual and practical point of view. However, in the context of the widespread ratification of TRIPs and the increasingly tenuous nature of farmers' hold over their resources and knowledge, it is necessary to go beyond criticism and understand the additional requirements of the current international legal system with respect to the needs of farmers and more broadly of food security for all individuals.

This chapter first looks at some of the reasons for introduction of plant variety protection and examines in particular the links with food security and the reasons for introducing plant variety protection measures. The second

---

2. See respectively Convention on Biological Diversity, Rio de Janeiro, 5 June 1992, and International Treaty on Plant Genetic Resources for Food and Agriculture, Rome, 3 Nov. 2001.

section surveys the property rights forms that have been proposed at the international level to provide plant variety protection and examines the existing legal regime in India with regard to plant variety protection. The third section argues that India needs to do more than it has done until now to implement a plant variety protection regime which truly fosters food security, provides traditional knowledge holders with secure property rights and rethinks farmers' rights in a broader context which takes into account the imperatives of food security and agro-biodiversity conservation alongside the already implemented focus on commercialization.

1. Plant Variety Protection and Food Security

Plant variety protection is intrinsically linked to food security. In fact, it can only be justified if it enhances food security. This section briefly explores the notion of food security before turning to the specific issue of plant variety protection.

A. Food Security

Food security can be understood at different level, from the household to the international level.[3] It is commonly held that at present there are sufficient food supplies at the international level[4] and in the Indian context at the national level as well.[5] However, studies indicate that with increases in population, and diminishing land availability, international and national food security will be a major concern in coming years.[6] To achieve food security at the national level states require sufficient resources to either produce or import enough food to feed the whole population and an efficient distribution

---

3. According to Paragraph 1 of the Plan of Action of the World Food Summit, Rome, 13-17 Nov. 1996, food security exists 'when all people, at all times, have physical and economic access to sufficient, safe and nutritious food to meet their dietary needs and food preferences for an active and healthy life'.
4. See, e.g., Carl F. Jordon, Genetic Engineering, the Farm Crisis and World Hunger 52 Bioscience 523, 526 (2002).
5. See, e.g. Indian Economic Survey, 2001-02 (2002).
6. See, e.g., Fao, The State of Food Insecurity in the World, 2002 (2002).

system to ensure everyone's access. Ensuring food security at the household level implies that people must either have sufficient income to purchase food or the capacity to feed themselves directly by cultivating their own food.

Food security is directly linked to agro-biodiversity which is essential to promote resilience in farming. Reduction in diversity (through practices such as monoculture) increases vulnerability to natural forces, to pest/weed attack and other plant diseases.[7] Therefore, agro-biodiversity is of primary importance for small-holder and/or subsistence farmers as it ensure both income-generation and household food security. Agro-biodiversity also provides ecosystem services on farms, such as pollination, fertility and nutrient enhancement, and insect and diseases management and water retention and thus makes for more productive farming, decreasing the number of the external inputs required.[8] Additionally, agro-biodiversity provides the raw material (or the genetic pool) for all crop-related biotechnology research and development. Diversity also has nutritional and social importance, where different varieties may contain different nutrients and health benefits or may be of differing cultural worth.

Small-holder and traditional farmers have customarily practiced farming techniques which conserve and enhance agro-biodiversity. In order to maximize productivity and minimize risk they have made certain selections whereby they have preserved old varieties, invented new varieties and adapted existing varieties to suit their local environment, thereby enriching agro-biodiversity.[9] As a result, the promotion of such farming is relevant, not just for household food

---

7. See for instance, M.S. Swaminathan, Ethics and Equity in the Use and Collection of Plant Genetic Resources: Some Issues and Approaches in International Plant Genetic Resources Institute, Ethics and Equity in Conservation and Use of Genetic Resources and Sustainable Food Security, 7 (1997).
8. Lori Ann Thrupp, Linking Agriculture biodiversity and Food Security: The Valuable Role of Agrobiodiversity for Sustainable Agriculture, 76, International Affairs 265, 268 (2000).
9. See, J. Esquinas-Alcazar, 'The Realisation of Farmers' Rights', in M.S. Swaminathan (ed.), Agro-biodiversity and Farmers' Rights 2 (1996).

security, but also for guaranteeing food security at national and international levels as well. It is essential therefore, that farmers retain control over plant varieties so that they may continue to innovate, improve and adapt varieties to suit changing needs and conditions.[10] Additionally, since food security and access to food is also linked to adequate income, promotion of small-holder and labour-intensive farming is essential in developing countries like India, where a large percentage of people earn their livelihood from agricultural labour.

National policy plays a vital role in countering food insecurity. The principles emanating from the human right to food form an important basis for such a policy.[11] One of the State's obligations with respect to the human right to adequate food is that it must proactively engage in activities to strengthen people's access to and utilization of resources and means to ensure their livelihood and food security.[12] This includes measures such as land reform, ensuring physical and economic access to credit, natural resources, new technologies, rural infrastructure, irrigation, and provision of explicit farmers' rights through legislation. Rigorous monitoring and planning by the State is required to ensure that cash crops do not replace food crops at the cost of food security. The State must also regulate private sector activities to ensure that they do not impinge on the resources of people who do not have access to sufficient food (which includes ensuring that private sector firms do not intrude on Farmers' Rights and that their activities sufficiently promote agro-biodiversity).[13] The State

10. See, e.g., objectives 3.1 and 3.4(d) of the Plan of Action supra n. 3.
11. The human right to adequate food has found expression in various international documents. See, e.g., Art. 11 of the International Covenant on Economic, Social and Cultural Rights, New York, 16 Dec. 1996.
12. Paragraph 15, Committee on Economic, Social and Cultural Rights, General Comment No. 12—The Right to Adequate Food (Art. 11), UN Doc. E/C.12/1999/5 (1999). [hereafter General Comment on Article 11].
13. In fact failure by the State to regulate individuals or groups so as to prevent them from violating the right to food amounts to a violation of its obligations (see Paragraph 19 of the General Comment on Article 11, *Supra* n. 12).

must also ensure that there is sufficient R&D in the area of under-utilised crops of high nutritional value.[14]

B. Law and Policy Rationale for Plant Variety Protection

At the outset, it must be mentioned that plant variety protection can have a narrow and broad meaning. The narrow view only considers plant variety protection from the point of view of commercial breeders and the needs of the biotechnology industry. The broader view acknowledges that there are different actors in plant variety management who deserve protection and who perform different functions, ranging from innovation (new seeds) to agro-biodiversity management.

India has had a number of reasons for introducing a plant variety protection regime. The most immediate trigger for the Plant Variety Act 2001 are the obligations undertaken in the WTO context, specifically under Article 27.3.b of TRIPs Agreement. Article 27.3.b of TRIPs imposes on all countries the introduction of some form of intellectual property protection for plant varieties. However, it does not impose the introduction of patents and therefore leaves member states free to devise their own legal framework in this regard (*sui generis* option). While WTO membership imposed a specific deadline on India for the introduction of plant variety protection, other factors are also at play. India has, for instance, been subjected several times to the appropriation of local knowledge through patents in foreign countries (also referred to as biopiracy) in the past few years. While the introduction of intellectual property rights in the field of genetic engineering may not provide a direct counter to biopiracy, it raises the profile of traditional knowledge as an issue worthy of debate and protection. Beyond issues specifically linked to biopiracy, the development of an intellectual property rights regime related to plant varieties is generally reflective of boarder trends towards the appropriation through private property rights of resources and knowledge previously deemed to be freely available to all individuals and nations. The trend towards

14. Objective 3.4, Plan of Action, *Supra* n. 3.

privatization of resources, knowledge and means of production has been tremendous in the past couple of decades. It finds expression in the field of agriculture with the progressive development of an international legal framework, which favours private ownership of genetically modified seeds over public access, and sharing of knowledge. This has, for instance, been reflected at the national level with the increase in incentives given to the private sector seed industry.[15]

Plant variety protection can be justified by necessity, or in other words by WTO membership. Other substantive reasons also help justifying plant variety protection both from the perspective of commercial breeders, farmers and agro-biodiversity conservation. As far as commercial breeders are concerned, the rationale for the introduction of plant variety protection is that it will promote food security because genetic engineering offers humankind its only chance to significantly increase yields in coming decades in view of the shortage of arable land to produce more food for an expanding population. Interestingly, the enhancement of food security is also an argument which can be used to justify Farmers' Rights on farmers' varieties since protection include the role that farmers play in sustainably using biodiversity and specifically in developing, conserving and enhancing agricultural biodiversity.

Within this general framework, several possibilities are open to the government. It can choose to protect only commercial breeders with the introduction of patents and be fully in compliance with its TRIPs obligations. It may choose to introduce plant breeders' rights and thereby provide rights which include some exceptions in favour of other breeders and farmers. It may further choose to grant rights only to breeders but introduce a benefit-sharing scheme which for instance, takes into account its obligations under the Biodiversity Convention. Finally, it can go beyond the preceding options and protect all relevant actors in the field of agricultural. management, from farmers to local communities and panchayats to commercial breeders and state governments, an

15. Seed Policy, 1988.

approach which takes into account not only TRIPs obligations but also all other relevant international treaties.

2. Legal Framework for Plant Variety Protection and Management

The legal framework for plant variety protection includes the different treaties that India has ratified in this field and the different legislative instruments adopted to implement international commitments.

A. *International Legal Framework*

India has taken different kinds of commitments in the field of plant variety protection and management. These include a series of obligations concerning the conservation and sustainable use of biological resources as well as commitments concerning the protection of traditional knowledge and Farmers' Rights and a series of obligations in the field of intellectual property rights regarding the commercial use of plant varieties.

Firstly, India has ratified the Biodiversity Convention which provides the basic framework for the conservation and the use of biological resources. It affirms India's sovereignty over its biological resources but qualifies India's control with the introduction of the notion of 'common concern' which implies that the protection of biodiversity in India is of interest not only to this country but also to the international community at large. The Biodiversity Convention is noteworthy for recognizing the need to conserve while also acknowledging the legitimacy of using biological resources which provide, for instance, every individual's basic food needs. The Convention also provides that governments must preserve traditional knowledge and foster its application.[16] While this provision does not mandate the recognition of the rights of traditional knowledge holders, it provides at least the lineaments of a policy framework in this regard. The Convention also regulates access to biological resources and the sharing of benefits arising from their use. It attempts to

16. Art 8j of the Biodiversity Convention.

provide a framework which respects donor countries' sovereign rights over their biological and genetic resources while facilitating access by users. Access must therefore be provided on 'mutually agreed terms' and is subject to the 'prior informed consent' of the country of origin.[17] Further, the convention provides that donor countries of micro-organisms, plants or animals used commercially have the right to obtain a fair share of the benefits derived from use. Finally, the Convention constitutes one of the few treaties which offer a specific statement on the relationship between the management of biological resources and intellectual property rights. Article 16 clearly indicates that intellectual property rights are not to undermine the working of the Convention.

Secondly, India has also ratified the PGRFA Treaty. This treaty adopts to a large extent the philosophy of the Biodiversity Convention and provides for the three interrelated goals of conservation, sustainable use and benefit sharing.[18] The overall aims of the Treaty are the promotion of sustainable agriculture and food security. The Treaty is significant for radically altering the legal status of plant genetic resources in international law. While the previous instrument—the 1983 International Undertaking[19]—promoted the sharing of plant genetic resources, the new Treaty affirms states' sovereign rights over their PGRFA and condones the introduction of intellectual property rights. One of the main contributions of the PGRFA Treaty to the international legal framework is its focus on the situation of farmers, their contribution to the conservation of agro-biodiversity, the rights they have over their physical assets—for instance, seeds—and to a much lesser extent the question of traditional knowledge. More specifically, the PGRFA Treaty gives recognition to farmers' contribution to conserving and enhancing plant genetic resources for food and agriculture. It further gives broad guidelines to states concerning the scope of the rights to be protected under this

17. Art. 15 of the Biodiversity Convention.
18. Art. 1 of the PGRFA Treaty.
19. International Undertaking on Plant Genetic Resources, Res. 8/83, Report of the Conference of FAO, 22nd Sess., Rome, 5-23 Nov. 1983, Doc. C83/REP.

heading but overall devolves the responsibility for realizing Farmers' Rights to member states. This includes the protection of traditional knowledge, farmers' entitlement to a part of benefit-sharing arrangements and the right to participate in decision-making regarding the management of plant genetic resources. However, the treaty is silent with regard to farmers' rights over their landraces. In fact, the 'recognition' of farmers' contribution to plant genetic resource conservation and enhancement does not include any property rights. In this context, the only rights that are recognized are the residual rights to save, use, exchange and sell farm-saved seeds. The overall significance of the PGRFA Treaty lies in the fact that it is the first treaty providing a legal framework which not only recognizes the need for conservation and sustainable use of plant genetic resources for food and agriculture but also delineates a regime for access and benefit sharing and in this process provides direct and indirect links to intellectual property right instruments.

Thirdly, India was a founding member of the WTO and in this capacity must implement the TRIPs Agreement. TRIPs generally provides minimum levels of intellectual property rights protection in all member states. This has brought about a substantial burden of adjustment in the patents field because the Patents Act, 1970 differed in significant respects from what was required under TRIPs. Among the many changes that India has had to bring in, the introduction of plant variety protection called for by Article 27.3.b of TRIPs has given rise to significant debate because of the choice it offers between adopting patents or a *sui generis* system. This choice has often been interpreted as implying that all countries either have to introduce patents or plant breeders' rights closely related to patents which were first defined in the UPOV Convention.[20] These rights grant commercial breeders exclusive rights over their inventions but include more exceptions than patents, and in particular can include exceptions in favour of other breeders' research and in favour of farmers. While PBRs

20. International Convention for the Protection of New Varieties of Plants, Paris, 2 Dec. 1961, as Revised at Geneva on 10 Nov. 1972, 23 Oct. 1978 and 19 Mar. 1991 (UPOV Doc. 221(E), 1996).

constitute one alternative to patents, the *sui generis* option is not limited to PBRs and can be construed in a number of different ways, thereby allowing countries to devise a plant variety protection regime which fits their specific needs and situation while taking their other obligations into account. The inclusion of the *sui generis* option is therefore of great significance within TRIPs because it allows member-states to explore alternatives to patents beyond what Articles 7 and 8 allow.[21]

Overall, the international legal framework in the field of plant variety protection and management is characterized by it lack of cohesion. While on the one hand, the Biodiversity Convention and the PGRFA Treaty attempt to provide answers to the relationship between intellectual property rights and environment, the TRIPs Agreement addresses intellectual property rights issues without taking into account concerns regarding environmental conservation or the management of traditional knowledge. Given that there is no international institution to ensure that different negotiations produce compatible treaties, the cohesion of different international obligations with each other must be mostly judged at the level of their implementation.[22] This is why close scrutiny of implementation legislations is imperative to ensure that all international obligations are given similar importance, with the exception of fundamental rights which by constitutional mandate ought to be given more prominence that the rest.

B. *Domestic Legal Framework*

India is one of the first countries in the world to have evolved an intellectual property rights legislation simultaneously granting rights to both breeders and farmers.

21. Arts. 7 and 8 provide the broader framework within which the TRIPS Agreement must be understood and implemented and may constitute the legal basis for exceptions in favour of developing countries.
22. The Convention on the Law of Treaties, Vienna, 23 May 1969, provides the basic framework for interpreting treaties, and includes provisions concerning the interpretation of different treaties addressing similar issues. It provides, for instance, that states must implement all their international obligations in good faith.

The protection of plant varieties and Farmers' Rights Act, 2001, establishes a unique system by extending the concept of plant Breeders' Rights (PBRs) currently applied to new varieties of breeders, to varieties held by the farmers, NGOs, and public sector institutions. The law emerged from a process that attempted to incorporate the interests of various stakeholders, including private sector breeders, public sector institutions, non-governmental organizations and farmers, within the property rights framework. The Protection of Plant Varieties and Farmers' Rights Act, 2001 (Act 53 of 2001) constitutes the government's response to its obligations under Article 27.3.b of the TRIPs Agreement. The Act focuses on the establishment of plant breeders' rights and farmers' rights. The regime for plant breeders' rights largely follows the model provided by UPOV and the criteria for registration are the same as those found in UPOV, namely novelty, distinctness, uniformity and stability. The Act incorporates elements from the 1978 version of UPOV and includes some elements from the more stringent 1991 version such as the possibility to register essentially derived varieties.

The second main aim of the Act is the introduction of farmers' rights. At this level, substantial changes were proposed by the Joint Parliamentary Committee to which the Bill was referred after its introduction in Parliament.[23] While the original version of the Bill introduced in Parliament only contained a short provision on farmers' rights, the Committee decided to add a whole new chapter on farmers' rights. As adopted, the Act seeks to put farmers' rights on a par with breeders' rights. It provides, for instance, that farmers can, like commercial breeders, apply to have a variety registered.[24] Generally speaking, the Act envisages that farmers should be treated like commercial breeders and should receive the same kind of protection for the varieties they develop.

23. See Joint Committee on the Protection of Plant Varieties and Farmers' Rights Bill, 1999, Report of the Joint Committee (August 2000).

24. Section 16(1)(d) of the Protection of Plant Varieties And Farmers' Rights Act, 2001.

The Act provides two different channels for benefit sharing Section 26 and Section 41[25] both provide opportunities for receiving financial compensation. The main difference between the two is that Section 41 specially targets village communities and provides less stringent procedural conditions. Thus, it neither provides a time frame nor specifies that claimants should pay a fee. In both cases, it is significant that the Authority has significant discretion in disposing of the benefit-sharing claims. Surprisingly, Section 41 comes closer to recognizing the intellectual contribution of the benefit claimers than Section 26. The former provides that claims can be made concerning the contribution to the evolution of a variety by a group while the latter only mentions the use of genetic material from the claimant variety as a basis for a claim. Further, while Section 26 requires the commercial utility and the demand for the variety in the market to be taken into account in the assessment of the claims, there is no such requirement under Section 41. The last major distinction is that Section 4 only provides for compensation to a community of individuals whereas a single person may benefit under Section 26. *Overall, the existence of two partly overlapping, partly different regimes for benefit sharing is likely to be the cause of much confusion on the part of benefit-claimers and is unlikely to foster their claims for compensation. At a conceptual level, two main critiques can be raised against these benefit-sharing regimes. First, they divert attention from the issue of providing property rights. Second, even in the limited sense of financial compensation, the burden of proof is on the claimants who finally remain dependent on the Authority's decisions.*

On the whole, the new elaborate section on farmers' rights is progressive but further rethinking of the conceptual framework of the Act would be required to provide fully effective farmers' rights. This is first due to the fact that farmers' rights were only added as an afterthought to a regime based on the UPOV Convention. The criteria for registration of varieties were not rethought and still exclusively reflect the needs of registration for commercial breeders. Second, benefit sharing as envisaged does not contribute to strengthening the

25. See Ss. 26 and 41 of the Plant Variety Act.

rights of farmers. It only fosters the recognition that actors who cannot apply for property rights should be offered some financial compensation.

The Biodiversity Act, 2002 addresses some questions which are relevant for biodiversity management in general and plant variety management specifically. The main focus of the Act is on the question of access to resources.[26] Its response to current challenges is to assert the country's sovereign rights over natural resources. It therefore proposes to put stringent limits on access to biological resources or related knowledge for all foreigners. The Act's insistence on sovereign rights reflects current attempts by various countries to assert control over the resources or knowledge they control. While the Act focuses on preserving India's interests *vis-a-vis* other states in rather strong terms, its main impact within the country will be to concentrate power in the hands of the government. Indeed, Indian citizens and legal persons must give prior intimation of their intention to obtain biological resources to the state biodiversity boards.[27] The Act is even more stringent in terms of intellectual property rights since it requires that all inventors obtain the consent of the National Biodiversity Authority before applying for such rights.[28] The impact of this clause is, however, likely to be limited since patent applications are covered by a separate clause.[29] Further, the Authority has no extra-territorial authority.

Overall, the Biodiversity Act implicitly takes the position that India cannot do more than regulate access by foreigners to its knowledge base. It does, however, attempt to discipline the intellectual property rights system in some respects. As noted, it requires inventors who want to apply for intellectual property rights to seek the Authority's permission. It also

26. The only substantive chapter of the Biological Diversity Act, 2002 (Act 18 of 2003)—Chapter II—is entitled Regulation of Access to Biological Diversity.
27. S. 7 of the Biological Diversity Act.
28. S. 6 of the Biological Diversity Act.
29. Permission of the National Biodiversity Authority must be obtained before the sealing of the patent but can be obtained after the acceptance of the patent by the patent authority. See Section 6.1 of the Biological Diversity Act.

authorizes the Authority to allocate a monopoly right to more than one actor. Further the Authority is also entitled to oppose the grant of intellectual property rights outside India.[30] The Act also seeks to address the question of the rights of holders of local knowledge by setting up a system of benefit sharing. The benefit sharing scheme is innovative insofar as it provides that the Authority can decide to grant joint ownership of a monopoly intellectual right to both the inventor and the Authority or the actual contributors if they can be identified.[31] However, the sharing of intellectual property rights is only one of the avenues that the Authority can choose by way of discharging of its obligation to determine benefit sharing. It is also in the Authority's power to allocate rights solely to itself or a contributor such as a farmer contributor. Other forms of benefit sharing include technology transfers, benefit claimers becoming associated with research and development or the location of production, research and development units in areas where this will facilitate better living standards to the benefit claimers.

Finally, plant variety protection is also influenced by the patent legislation. While the Patents Act as adopted in 1970 dealt with patents in general and was not specifically related to biological resources, it addressed a number of issues that are of relevance in the context of PGR management. It rejected,for instance the patentability of all methods of agriculture and was generally much more restrictive than similar laws in western countries. TRIPs has imposed significant alternations to this Act. The Patents (Amendment) Act, 2002 has generally modified the Act to allow compliance with TRIPs.[32] The Amendment Act brings the duration of the rights to a uniform 20-year period and also substantially modifies the sections concerning the working of the patents by, for instance, doing away with licences of rights. The provision which seeks to oblige patentees to manufacture their inventions in India was also struck out because of the TRIPs requirements that imports should not be treated differently from products locally

30. S. 18.4 of the Biological Diversity Act.
31. S. 21.2a of the Biological Diversity Act.
32. See Patents (Amendment) Act, 2002.

produced.[33] With regard to environmental protection, the Amendment Act includes some of the TRIPs exceptions related to environment and health. It also addresses the question of biopiracy by imposing the disclosure of the source and geographical origin of the biological material used in a patented invention. Further, non-disclosure of the geographical origin or the anticipation of the invention in local or indigenous knowledge constitutes grounds for opposing or revoking a patent.

3. Plant Variety Protection for Food Security

As noted above, there are a number of different actors involved in plant variety management, all with the ultimate aim of enhancing food security. Existing conditions indicate that while a significant segment of the overall population has easy access to sufficient food, there remain crores of people whose basic food needs are not met. In an economy where employment remains mostly in the agricultural sector, it is therefore of primary importance to make sure that the legal regime which is being set-up favours access to food for the majority of poor people and fosters farmers' control over their land, crops and knowledge. This section argues that the current legal regime does not go far enough towards empowering farmers. Further, on the basis of the new PGRFA Treaty it argues that a broader conception of farmers' rights should be adopted with a view to fosters farmers' hold over their knowledge and with a view to comprehensively implement all international obligations in this field.

1. Assessment of the Current Legal Regime

The legal framework put in place until now can be looked at from two completely different angles. On the one hand, the Indian Plant Variety Act is among the most progressive plant variety protection legislations adopted by a developing country in furtherance of its TRIPs obligations. The apparent will to provide equal rights to commercial breeders and farmers is farsighted insofar as it indicates a clear

33. Article 27 of the TRIPs Agreement.

understanding that the forces shaping globalisation require the assignment of property rights to all concerned actors in the different fields where appropriation is taking place. *In particular, it is noteworthy for providing a clear acknowledgement that farmers' rights can be conceived as intellectual property rights, in exactly the same way as other products of human creativity.* On the other hand, it appears quite likely that the chapter of farmers' rights will not be implemented. Firstly, farmers' rights were introduced as an afterthought to the first draft which contained only rudimentary farmers' rights. The Act provides only one set of criteria for registration—which are the criteria taken from the UPOV Convention for the protection of commercial breeders' varieties—and as a result, it will be extremely difficult for farmers to register their varieties even though they are entitled to it. Secondly, the decision of the Government to formally join UPOV will at least put pressure on the Plant Variety Authority to favour commercial breeders over farmers and at worst may lead to the Authority either formally or informally not implementing the provisions of the Act concerning farmers' rights. *As a result, though this Act theoretically recognises farmers' rights, a lot remains to be done for farmers' rights to become a reality in the form of intellectual property rights.* The protection of traditional knowledge is also taken up in the Biodiversity Act which focuses on the appropriation of Indian traditional knowledge by foreigners but does not empower holders of traditional knowledge with rights to stop unwanted appropriation within the country. Another shortcoming of the Plant Variety Act is that, though TRIPs compliant insofar as it provides for a *sui generis* option within the narrow confines of Article 27.3.b of TRIPs, it only deals with plant variety management from the point of view of their commercialization and fails to take into account the fact that commercial activities cannot be separated, either legally or in practice, from the conservation of agricultural biodiversity, the rights of farmers and that of the state.

Apart from the specific problems concerning farmers' rights, the current legal framework is fraught with inconsistencies which are linked to the different origins of the Acts. Each of the three legislatives instruments examined above have been individual responses to specific international obligations which have been addressed by different ministries and departments according to the main focus of the concerned treaty. *The result is a legal framework which lacks a sense of unity and purpose and instead comprises a collection of defensive responses to international commitments, rather than a cohesive strategy to address internal problems.* Consequently, there are, for instance, a number of overlaps between the benefit-sharing regimes proposed in the Biodiversity Act and the Plant Variety Act while the Patents Act does not even acknowledge the issue of benefit-sharing despite the fact that benefit-sharing is on the whole a direct consequence of the introduction of intellectual property rights in the agricultural field. Some of the other shortcomings of the PVPFR Act are as follows :

I. The PVP Act provides for farmers' rights and allows farmers to save, use, sow resow, exchange, share or sell his farm produce including seed of a variety protected under this Act in the same manner as he was entitled before the coming into force of this Act. But they are not allowed to sell branded seed of variety protected under this Act. And Branded seeds means 'any seed put in package or any other container and labeled in a manner indicating that such seed is of a variety protected under this Act'. Given case law in Plant Variety Protection, even "brown bagging" and farmers exchange has been treated as "commercial" sale by seed corporations. This clause could thus undermine farmers' rights rather than protect it, unless a genuinely independent *sui generis* law on farmers' rights is evolved.

II. The criteria for registration of extant varieties and farmers' varieties, however, is not entirely clear is the Act. The Act proposes that it would be based on distinctiveness uniformity and stability[34] as defined by the authority. The authority is yet to provide such definitions and this will be a crucial factor in

34. S15 of the Plant Variety Act, 2001.

determining whether farmers would actually be able to register their varieties.

III. *Monopolies over seed production*: Through the PVP Act, the Multinational Seed Companies are seeking total control of seed, the first link in the food chain and through control over seed, they control the food system. If all farmers who are the original breeders, could be forced into the market every year, the seed industry will have a $7.5 billion market.[35] The impact of the new seed law needs to be assessed in the context of the monopolies already in place in the industrialized countries. Even in India, where many companies seem to be making Bt. Cotton, the intellectual property rights to Bt. Gene are in the hand of one company, Monsanto.[36] IPRs on seed are thus creating seed monopolies. Not only is the seed industry gaining total control over seed supply, it is also getting increasingly concentrated. The PVP Act would prove to be an effective tool through which the consolidation of seed companies over Indian agriculture would be accomplished. The stronger the rights of TNCs, the weaker are the rights of farmers since it is the erosion of farmers' rights which create MNC's monopolies.

IV. "Benefit Sharing", as an instrument to undermine farmers' rights: The Act pays lip service to the idea of royalty payment to farmers when their varieties are used for breeding new variety through the mechanism of "benefit sharing". Instead of farmers' rights being recognized as collective, community rights derived from their having evolved traditional varieties collectively and cumulatively, benefit sharing replaces farmers' rights with rights of the seed industry, with farmers receiving a small payment. Which farmers will be paid and the

35. The need for genuine *Sui Generis* Law to defend Farmers Rights as Traditional breeders : Dr. V. Shiva and Afsar H. Jafri (From Internet, www.vshiva.net).

36. *Ibid.*, p. 5.

amount of payment is left to a District Magistrate. However, given the fact that farmers' varieties have been developed by millions of farmers across large geographical regions, it is difficult, even in well-structured system to identify the beneficiaries and distribute equitably the benefits among them. Moreover the system of benefit sharing is very unreliable. The benefit sharing is made subject to the commercial utility of the "new" derived variety.[37] Moreover the benefit will be recovered as an arrear of land revenue by the District Magistrate within whose jurisdiction the breeder liable for such benefits sharing resides.[38] However, seed corporations which control IPRs are not producers, hence this mechanism is flawed at its very roots. Since most of the seeds are being bred by the Multinational seed companies with their headquarter in a foreign land, in this case who would recover the benefit from the breeders? Moreover the benefit sharing is made subject to claim if any.[39] If no one makes claim for benefit sharing, there is no voluntary recognition of benefit sharing by the breeder or the Authority based on the passport data. Keeping in mind the literacy status of our farmers as well as the access to Government Gazzette, most of the cases of biopiracy would go unnoticed. The alternative is to recognize farmers as breeders and protect their community rights to their collective, cumulative innovation through a genuinely *sui generis* law made for protection of traditional knowledge.

V. Very Harsh Penalties for Farmers: While the breeders are provided with very strong protection, the Act provides for very harsh punishment to farmers (violators) for the infringement of breeders rights. The penalties are prescribed not only for copying the

37. S26(5)(b) of the Plant Variety Act, 2001.
38. S26(7) of the Plant Variety Act, 2001.
39. S26(2) of the Plant Variety Act, 2001.

packaging but also the registered name or denomination of the registered variety or giving their variety a denominaton deceptively similar to the registered variety.[40] The breeders' rights are so strong that even in the case of the slightest doubt of violation or infringement on the part of the breeders, the onus of proving the innocence is upon the alleged violators (farmers). Whether it is the case of demanding benefits for using their variety or for proving innocence for infringement of breeders' rights, the onus is put on the poor farming community. If a violator fails to prove that he acted in innocence, the penalty is very harsh which also includes jail term. If a person applies any false denomination to a variety or misrepresent the address of the breeder of a variety registered under this Act in course of trading such variety, he shall be punished with imprisonment for a term not less than three months but may extend to two years, or fine which shall not be less than fifty thousand rupees but which may extend to five lakh rupees, or both.[41] In case of repetition of violation, the minimum jail term is one year which may extend to three years and the fine form two lakhs which may extend to 20 lakhs rupees or both.[42] The rights of the farmers to claim benefit for use of their variety is very weak in comparison to the rights of the breeders for protection of their knowledge. Given the cases of biopiracy such as "basmati", "neem", "turmeric", etc. farmers cultivating their own varieties could be treated as violators given the reversal of burden of proof. The only safeguard is a *sui generis* law on traditional knowledge, which protects farmers' rights and their freedom to use their seeds and innovations without threat from corporate pirates. Corporations

40. S64 of the Plant Variety Act, 2001.
41. S70 of the Plant Variety Act, 2001.
42. S73 of the Plant Variety Act, 2001.

are misusing IPRs to criminalise innocent farmers as the case of Percy Schmeiser shows.[43]

VI. No Corporate liability, No Protection for Farmers against Seed Failure: The PVP Act 2001 does not provide any strong protection to the farmers in case of failure of registered varieties. In view of failure of Bt.Cotton, the farmers of Warangal suffered a loss of Rs. 16,657 per hectare[44] and no compensation was paid to the victim farmers as yet. The Act provides that "... if such propagating material fails to provide such performance under such given conditions as the farmer or the group of farmers or the organization of farmers, as the case may be, may claim compensation in the prescribed manner before the Authority and the Authority shall after giving notice to the breeder of the variety and after providing him an opportunity to file opposition in the prescribed manner and after hearing the parties, it may direct the breeder of the variety to pay such compensation as it deems fit, to the farmer or the group of farmers or the organization of farmers, as the case may be.[45] This protection is very weak and cannot act as a deterrent. The frequent seed failure and the suicides of farmers due to the loss of crops demands a severe punishment to the breeder in case of failure of their seeds or propagating materials. The absence of liability clause and the replacement of a locally accessible justice system by centralized Authority increases the power of seed corporations and robs the farmers of any reliable access to claims for compensation and holding corporation liable for seeds failure and false claims.

VII. *Very weak Researchers Rights*: The PVP Act seeks to restrict the rights of the researchers and broadens the rights of the plant breeders. Researchers have to take permission of the breeders for repeated use of a

43. Monsanto Canada Inc. *v.* Schmeiser, Supreme Court of Canada, Judgement dt. 21st May 2004 (2004) SCC 34.
44. *National Herald*, New Delhi, 9th June 2003.
45. S39(2) of Plant Variety Act, 2001.

protected variety as parental lines. It says : "the authorization of the breeder of a registered variety is required where the repeated use of such variety as a parental line is necessary for commercial production of such other newly developed variety". No breeder would ever authorize others for repeated use of his/her protected variety for commercial propagation. And no researcher would ever do research on a variety if he cannot commercialize it. Hence, the Act restricts the researchers' rights and grants extended monopoly to the breeder. The Act thus negates the right to free access to protected varieties for further development of new improved varieties, and also negates any true competitiveness, which would reduce the price of seeds.

2. The Need for a Broader Conception of Farmers' Rights

The preceding section indicates that there are some general and some specific problems in the adopted legal regime for plant variety management and protection. A number of these problems are of a technical nature and relate, for instance, to the lack of coordination between the different Acts. One more substantive issue is the question of farmers' rights or the rights of farmers over their traditional knowledge. The need to find a more comprehensive answer to this issue has been made more pressing with the ratification by India of the new PGRFA Treaty. The importance of this treaty is linked to the fact that it directly links biodiversity conservation, biodiversity use and farmers' rights and to the fact that it constitutes a direct response to the introduction of intellectual property rights in agriculture through patents and plant breeders' rights.

The existence of different treaties separately addressing plant variety management and protection makes their joint implementation an onerous task for member states. This process must, however, be undertaken because this is exactly what international law requires, and because this constitutes one important avenue to foster food security at all levels within the country.

Given that the emphasis at the international level has generally been on defining and strengthening the rights of exclusively commercially minded actors through patents and plant breeders' rights, the definition of a broader regime need not add much to existing and well-developed rights. It should rather focus on farmers' rights and the mainstreaming of biodiversity management and traditional knowledge protection. Starting with international obligations, the necessity to redraft farmers' rights to make them effective has been made more pressing following the ratification of the PGRFA Treaty. While the TRIPs agreement makes no mention of the necessity to protect farmers' rights, the PGRFA Treaty—while not defining farmers' rights at the international level—specifically puts the onus on member states to make farmers' rights a reality.[46] A few of the substantive elements that make up farmers' rights are indicated in the Treaty. These include, the protection of traditional knowledge, equitable benefit sharing, and the right to participate in decisions concerning the management of plant genetic resources. In other words, the Treaty steers countries towards recognizing the need for giving farmers control over their knowledge for reasons of justice as well as to foster sustainable use and conservation of plant genetic resources. However, it leaves member-states free to decide on the most appropriate framework for the same. There are a number of other elements in the PGRFA Treaty which point the direction for further work in the area, both in domestic and international law. The access and benefit-sharing regime instituted under the PGRFA Treaty is, for instance, much more developed and comprehensive than the one under the Biodiversity Convention. The PGRFA Treaty also indirectly highlights that it is difficult to distinguish biological resources, genetic resources and related knowledge. Indeed, the definition of genetic resources under the Treaty includes reproductive and vegetative propagating material that contains functional units of heredity.[47] More broadly, the Treaty links plant genetic resource conservation, intellectual property rights, sustainable agriculture and food security.

46. Art. 9.2 of the PGRFA Treaty.
47. Art. 2 of the PGRFA Treaty.

4

Moving from PVP to Plant Patents

1. INTRODUCTION

In the context of developing countries, PVP has been there for some time but patent for Plants is a recent Phenomenon. As Table 4.1 shows both Patent and PVP Provide exclusive monopoly rights over a creation for commercial Purposes over a Period of time. A Patent is a right granted to an inventor to prevent all others from making, using, and/or selling the patented invention for 15-20 years. The criteria for a Patent are novelty, inventiveness (non-obviousness), utility, and reproducibility. Although Patents were designed for industrial application, with biotechnology, patent offices now grant patents on microorganisms and, in some countries on all life forms.

The intellectual property regime for plant variety protection emerged with a strong commitment for public interest in mind. The whole Provision for compulsory licensing was introduced with this intention only. Under this Provision of compulsory licensing a holder of plant breeders' rights can neither refuse any applicant nor can offer unreasonable terms for this. Plant variety protection has worked well as a mechanism to promote the interests of the Plant breeders for developing new varieties through giving them Proprietary right on the one hand and as a custodian of public rights of access and use of genetic material on the other hand. PVP gives patent-like rights to plant breeders. What gets protected in this case is the genetic make-up of a specific plant variety. The criteria for protection are different: novelty, distinctness, uniformity and stability. PVP laws can provide exemptions for breeders, allowing them to save seeds from their harvest in plant breeding, thus PVP is the weaker sister of patenting mainly because of these exemptions. PVR also encourages cross-licensing between a holder of PVR and a holder of a patent. Under the breeders' exemption of plants variety rights anyone may use protected material for breeding purposes. However, the patent regime does not reciprocate this.

As Table 4.1 shows, in the patent regime the interpretation of research exemption is much narrower than that of the breeders' exemption in PVR. Thus, for instance, if a breeder wants to produce a new variety and needs a compulsory cross-licensee from a patent holder, the breeder has to demonstrate that the breeding programme will produce a technical progress, but all results of a breeding programme take a long span of research and development effort, so how can we demonstrate the technical progress right in the beginning? Thus cross-licensing for a plant breeder hardly means anything.[1] *Thus for all practical purposes PVR ends up protecting small advances in the breeding process while patent regime would actually lead the protection of bigger leaps in technological achievements.*

In Europe, animal and plant varieties have always been excluded form patentability under Article 53(b) of the European Patent Convention (EPC). This convention was

1. Similarly, if an application of PVR is made for a variety that contains a patented gene, is the actual making of the application an infringement of the patent? Obviously, the reply would be in affirmation and PVR can not be granted to the plant varieties containing patented gene, if the patent holder does not agree.

TABLE 4.1

Agreement on Trade Related Aspects of Intellectual Property (TRIPs), US Utility Patent Protection, The European Patent Convention (EPC) and the International Convention on the Protection of New Varieties of Plants (UPOV)

	TRIPs Agreement	*US Utility Patent*	*European Patent Convention*	*UPOV Convention 1991*
(1)	*(2)*	*(3)*	*(4)*	*(5)*
Granting Criteria	Novelty, Inventive step and Industrial Applicability	Novelty, Non-obviousness, Utility	Novelty, Inventive Step, Industrial Application	New, Distinct, Uniform and Stable
Industrial Applicability/ Utility	Not defined	Advantage over the Prior act	The invention must be capable of industrial application—this includes agricultural use but does not include methods of human treatment	Not a requirement
Distinctness	Not defined as a requirement for the sui *generis* system of protection mandated for plant varieties under Article 27(3)(b)	Not a requirement	Not a requirement	The verities must be clearly distinguishable in its essential characteristics from other varictics, which are a matter of common knowledge (e. g.

(Contd.)

TABLE 4.1 (Contd.)

(1)	(2)	(3)	(4)	(5)
				protected by a plant variety right) at the time of application.
Extent of Protection	(a) Where the subject matter of the patent is a product the rights allows the holder to prevent third parties, not having the consent of the holder using, offering for sale, selling or importing the product. (b) Patent holder can deny usage of the process he has developed or even the sale of product of that process.	(a) Right to prevent all others from using the invention. (b) Protection extends to all biological materials, genes to genotype.	(a) Right to prevent all others from using the invention (b) board claims are not permitted. (c) Protection extends to all biological materials, genes to genotype and includes plant groupings but not plant variety.	(a) Right to produce, reproduce, sale or stock any plant variety. (b) Right to extends to harvested material and other products obtained from material of the variety provided
Farmer Privilege	Not specific but possibly permitted via Article 30	Not permitted	Not permitted	Optional Contracting Parties may, within reasonable limits and subject to the

				safeguarding of the legitimate interests of the breeders' rights in the relation to any variety in order to permit farmers to use for propagating purposes
Breeders'/ Research Exemption	Not specific but possibly permit via Article 30	Free use of protected material for research purposes is permitted but only where it is for non-commercial purposes.	No-but such an exemption is usually provided in the national patent laws of Member States of the EPC.	Yes-non-infringing act include : (a) acts done privately and for non-commercial purposes (b) acts done for experimental purpose and for breeding
Compulsory Licenses	Yes, but only where (a) the applicant has requested for and been refused a licence from the patent holder (b) the use for which	No, although the ability of the patent of the patent holder (the licensor) to dictate the terms of any lincence s/he chooses to grant are		Not mentioned as such Article 17 states that : (1) Except where expressly provided in this Convention, non-Contracting Party may restrict

(Contd.)

TABLE 4.1 (Contd.)

(1)	(2)	(3)	(4)	(5)
	the applicant wishes to use the protected invention is non-exclusive (c) the use is predominantly within the domestic market (d) the licence holder pays an adequate remuneration. Where the license is needed in order to exploit a second patented invention which is depended then a license will be granted only where (1) the invention claimed in the second patent involves an important technical advance of considerable	subject to extensive restrictions via the common law doctrine of patent misuse and anti-trust laws		the free exercise of a breeders' right for reasons other than of public interest (2) When any such restriction has the effect of authorizing a third party to perform any act for which the breeders' authorization is required, the Contracting Party concerned shall take all measures necessary to ensure that the breeder receives equitable remuneration.

economic significance in relation to the invention claimed in the first patent;

(2) the owner or the first patent is entitled to a cross-licence on reasonable terms to use the invention claimed in the second patent; and

(3) the use in respect of the first patent is non-assignable except with the assignment of the second patent.

Each case is assessed on its individual merits, it is non-assignable, it is subject to termination when the circumstances change and any secession is subject to judicial review

(Contd.)

Table 4.1 (*Contd.*)

(1)	(2)	(3)	(4)	(5)
Duration of Protection	20 years from the date of filling	20 years from the date of filling	20 years from the date of filling	30 years for trees and vine, 25 years for all other varieties (Article 19)

Source : US Department of Agriculture Economics Research Service (1998).

signed in 1973. The term 'variety' was not defined in the EPC. As plant varieties could be protected either through the existing national law (plant breeders' right) or through the UPOV convention. With this, European patent office started establishing the fact that plant varieties fall under the jurisdiction of the patent regime. One of the major reasons sited for slow growth of biotechnology industry in Europe is the lack of certainty concerning intellectual property protection for biotechnology inventions.[2] The proponents of biotechnology suggest that the conflicts between the ethical aspects of technology development *vis-a-vis* commercial gains from technology have not allowed the growth of this industry. The Novartis decision (decision GO1/98) seems to confirm this. The decision suggests that plant varieties are not patentable but patent on a genus is possible. The genus is made up of species and sub-species and varieties. This mean that patents control of varieties is acquired through the proprietary control of genus. In the Novartis case, at issue, were the claims to plants containing a gene conferring resistance to plant pathogens. The Technical Board of Appeal referred the question to the Enlarged Board of Appeal.[3]

The Board found that a claim in which plant varieties are not claimed is not excluded from patentability under Article 53(b), even though it may embrace plant varieties. The Board further concluded that inventions ineligible for protection under the plant breeders' rights system were intended to be patentable under the European Patent Convention if they met all the other requirements of Patentability.

However, a directive from European Community on the protection of biotechnology inventions (directive 98/44 EC) contains specific provisions on the patentability of genetically engineered biological material including plants and animals. This marks a major departure from earlier practice in the European Union. The directive was adopted by the European Union on July 6, 1998 and all the necessary amendments were rectified by the EU on September 1, 1999. The most significant feature of the directive is the provision pertaining to the

2. *The Economist* (1997).
3. Blöchlinger (2000).

patentability of the biological material including inventions relating to plant and animal varieties, human body and sequences or partial sequences of genes.[4] The individual member-states of the EU have two years to amend their national laws to bring them into conformity with this directive.[5] The explanatory notice published in the OJ EPO records that since the early 1980s, the EPO has received about 15,000 applications in the field of biotechnology, for which about 3,000 patents have been granted. 1,500 applications relate to transgenic plants 600 to transgenic animals and 2000 to DNA sequences. The biotech directive had to be implemented into national law by July 30, 2000.

Germany has demanded that this directive is inadequate for promotion of biotechnology and in order to retain competitiveness of European biotechnology industry the directive should be further strengthened and tightened up. Most of the implementation was done by the UK through the Statutory Instrument (SI) 2000/2037. UK law is largely compatible with the biotech directive already. UK is attempting some balancing act between PVP and patents. There were one or two areas where changes are required. In particular, there needed to be introduced, into the patent law, derogations, equivalent to the derogations in the plant varieties legislation, to enable farmers to save and use seed on their own farms. A cross-licensing provision also needed to be introduced to both acts between plant variety rights and patent rights where the invention or plant variety constitutes 'significant technical progress' over the other right and could not be exploited without infringing the protection conferred on the other right holder. 'Significant technical progress' is a high hurdle to overcome. This part of the directive is still to be implemented. Although these compulsory license provisions are proposed to give recompense to the other rights holders, they also require

4. Erratt and Sechley (2000). The European Biotechnology Directive and the Patentability of Higher Life Forms. Canadian Biotechnology, 2000.
5. This directive has already been challenged in European Court of Justice by the Netherlands and Italy. For details, please refer www.greenpeace.org

the applicant for the compulsory license to cross-license its own rights to the person from whom it is seeking the compulsory license.[6] The UK SI has produced new schedules in order to ensure uniformity between the UK patent legislation and the biotech directive, the Patents Act and Rules to set out clearly the provisions of the biotech directive in national legislation. There is minor tinkering with the patents Act itself and the government is taking this opportunity to ensure compliance with Trade in Counterfeit Goods-part of the last round of the General Agreement on Tariffs and Trade, and the recent changes to the EPC.

2. EMERGENCE OF UTILITY PATENTS

In the US extension of IPRs to new plant varieties and biological inventions, including the development of biotechnologies, has stimulated private companies to invest in plant breeding. The Plant Patent Act of 1930 and the Plant Variety Protection Act (PVPA) of 1970 established plant breeders' rights for new plants and plant varieties. In 1980, a Supreme Court decision (Diamond *vs.* Chakraborty) authorized the use of patents for biological inventions, specifically microorganisms. Several recent decisions by the patent and Trademark office broadened the use of patents for plants and created space for utility patents (*ex prate* Hibberd in 1985) and animals (*ex prate* Allen in 1987). Utility patents are for any "new and useful process machine, manufacture, composition of matter or any new and useful improvement therefor". Utility patents can protect all the parts of the plants including genes, seeds' physiological and physical traits. As Table 4.1 shows utility patents have a larger coverage than PVPs in the sense that they cover not just a single variety as in PVPs but also all other varieties having same traits and functional properties. Further, in utility patent not only a single claim is allowed but it also provides protection for covering plant parts including flowers, fruits and cutting, etc. Apart from this, protection is not dependent on whether the plant is sexually produced or asexually produced.

6. Pharamalicensing (2001).

As a result, private sector research expenditures for plant breeding have increased from $ 6 million in 1960 to $ 400 million in 1992.[7] Nearly 70 percent of private sector plant breeding research expenditures in 1989 was for corn, and soybean. Private firms have also reacted to changes in IPRs by investing heavily in biotechnology techniques.

The number of plant patents, plant variety protection certificates (PVPC's) and Utility patents issued over the last 25 years has risen (Figure 4.1). The PVPA stimulated the development of new field crop varieties. By the end of 1994, 3,306 PVPC's had been issued for new crop varieties. The number of PVPC's issued for new varieties of field crops, grasses, and vegetables climbed up from 153 in 1971-74 to 992 in 1991-94. New soybean, corn and vegetable varieties accounted for 56 percent of total PVPC's awarded. The private sector own approximately 87 percent of the total PVPC's

FIG. 4.1
Trends in IPR in US

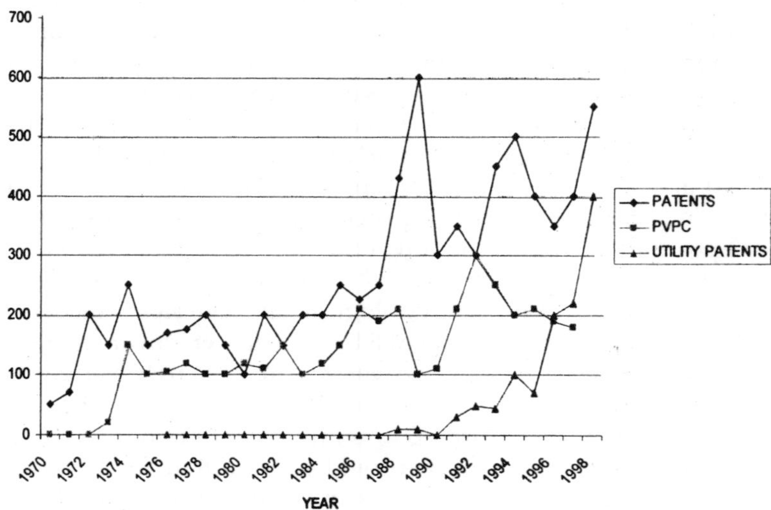

Source : USDAER (2000).

7. Klotz, Fugile and Pray, 1995, Fugile, Klotz and Gill, 1995.

issued. Oats was the only crop of which the public sector held a higher share of PVPC's. However, utility patents are the most difficult to obtain and have been awarded primarily for new biotechnology innovations, such as genetically engineered varieties. The number of utility patents issued has grown up very rapidly in the US. By December 1994, 324 utility patents had been issued for new plants or plant parts and 38 were issued for animals. As with PVPC's most utility patents were awarded to the private sector.[8] Thus, IPR has encouraged the private sector to develop new agricultural technologies by enabling firms to capture greater share of the commercial value of their inventions.

3. PATENTING OF RESEARCH TOOL

One of the major trends in the patenting which is emerging in US patent system is their broad nature. At times, it is even encompassing research tools necessary for further downstream research and development. Some of the research tools, patenting of which have attracted attention are expressed sequence tags (ESTs), restriction enzymes, screening systems, technique related to DNA sequencing and single nucleotide polymorphisms (SNPs).[9] As these research tools by definition have the power to control the downstream research of pharmaceuticals. They can wield an extremely large influence when patented. The problem of broad patenting is actually grown over the years. For instance, Agracetus patent on all transgenic cotton (US patent 5,159,135) or similar patents on all transgenic soybean. Some of these patents are subject to re-examination or litigation to determine their validity. Similarly, a new US patent awarded to Monsanto in 2001, giving an exclusive monopoly right on crucial method identifying modified plant cells in laboratory, US patent No. 6,174,724 covers all practical methods of making transformed plants that employ antibiotic resistance markers. The technique has been used in virtually all commercial GM crops. An earlier patent granted to another major US firm, Syngenta, covered a marker,

8. Fugile, Klotz and Gill, 1995.
9. Hirai (2001).

which enables plants cell transformation and selection without the use of antibiotic resistance marker. This technology was first developed in a very small firm Danisco in Denmark. This company sold the patent to Sandoz in 1998, which later became Novartis, which in 2000 became Syngenta.[10]

These issues can give rise to several policy challenges when seen in the context of developing countries. It may just foreclose entry of the late comers in the technology race, which would eventually affect public sector research endeavours, as is mostly practiced in the developing countries. While when seen in larger context of investment in research in developing such techniques, patents seems to be the only way to recover the investment. However, the need seems to be to analyse the research trends in the overall context of social requirement as with individual technological features of research tools, the scope of the technology and its contribution to society may differ. For instance, in developing countries ensuring a higher crop yield for adequate food supply would always be a priority over the necessity of developing a drug required for life style diseases.

The problem of EST patents having severe implications for future progress of genomic industries is also being seriously analysed in Japan. The opinion which is emerging there, suggests that, the utility of ESTs will not be recognized from the mere disclosure of a general function, i.e. capability of use as a research tool and such EST inventions will not be patented.[11] However, utility of EST can be recognized if it can be used as a probe for a gene encoding a specific useful protein or that it can be used as a tool to diagnose a specific disease.

The post-Green Revolution, agriculture production scenario seems to pose several challenges for food security in developing countries. It is high time that agricultural R and D plans prioritise investment on new technologies so as to rightly balance or rather supplement the traditional techniques with new technologies such as biotechnology. However, the opinion about biotechnology among the developing countries is mixed.

10. Genet (2001).
11. Hiraki (2000).

There are experts who actually enlist several factors why biotechnology per se, is not the right technology to ensure food security and reduce poverty in the developing countries. They even go up to the extent of saying that biotechnology is a technology that has been shaped by a narrow range of private interests—interests that are incompatible with the demands of an ecologically sound and socially—just agriculture.

Thus the issues that the advent of this technology raises, covers a much wider canvass. The ethical dimension of the genetically modified organisms (GMOs) have further confounded the ongoing confusion on the relevance of biotechnology for the developing countries. In the last decade or so, the transnational corporations have emerged as a major source of biotechnology products. This trend has, probably, further contributed to the concerns among the developing countries amidst growing reports about bio-piracy. These concerns have hot reflected in the wider debate being initiated to assess the relevance of this technology for developing countries.

In such a scenario, it may not be entirely misplaced, to observe that, since biotechnology is a frontier technology, upcoming in a dynamic international environment, it probably requires an altogether different approach to ensure the growth of the technology along with the desired socio-economic goals. Thus it poses a two-fold challenge, on one hand, the growth of technology has to be ensured and on the other, policies would have to be evolved not only to restrict its adverse implications but also for ensuring growth in the agricultural sector. Any imbalance between the two may offset the wider developmental impetus, which the agricultural sector needs at this point.

The WTO TRIPs regime Article 27.3(b) refers to have either a patent regime or an effective *sui generis* system for protection of plant varieties. In last decade or so, the developing countries have strongly debated the various aspects of *sui generis* system and what actually constitutes it. However, as is evident from the earlier sections the varietial protection is being attempted through much more stronger patent regime, which do not allow any kind of exemption and is much narrower in its scope than plant patents or plant variety protection. There is a continuous growth in what is called the utility patents in the US while the Biotechnology Directive of EU has suggested a similar mechanism for the protection of biotechnological inventions in Europe. Along with this there is also a growing trend of patenting the research tools as well. Thus in light of the developments in biotechnology the profile of patent regime is fast changing in the developed countries. Needless to mention that a large part of this research is emanating from the private sector.

These changes would have severe implications for the developing countries. More so when they are already struggling with the implementational hurdles of the TRIPs regime. There are many developing countries, including India, which have yet to put in place national legislations to position themselves *vis-a-vis* international negotiations at the WTO. India has come out with several drafts of biodiversity and patent laws but they have yet to see light of the day. There have been several reasons for this delay but now it seems to be clear that it would not only adversely affect the access to technology *per se* but the patenting of research tools would also exclude the late comers in the technology race from imitation or even from product development in any other form.

In this context, the role of public research institutions becomes very relevant. In developing countries productivity levels have yet to move anyway closer to the ones achieved in the developed countries. This requires not only the continuation of all budgetary support for the public research institutions in the developing countries but if required even increasing them to meet the demand. It is also important to ensure that public plant breeders/laboratories have access to the best science and germplasm. Similarly, capacity in public plant breeding should be enhanced. This increased capacity should be directed towards those crops, which are not likely to attract private investment. Over last so many years public plant breeding programmes have evolved with a free exchange of germplasm and cooperative scientific endeavors.

5

Traditional Knowledge as Prior Art in the Patent System

1. DEFINITION AND THE IMPORTANCE OF TRADITIONAL KNOWLEDGE

There is no agreed definition for "traditional knowledge". WIPO, in its fact finding mission report, uses the term "traditional knowledge" to refer to "...tradition-based literary, artistic or scientific works; performances; inventions; scientific discoveries; designs; marks; names and symbols; undisclosed information; and all other tradition-based innovations and creations resulting from intellectual activity in the industrial, scientific, literary or artistic fields.[1] WIPO also suggests that

1. One important and widely acknowledged aspect about traditional knowledge is that it does not imply static nor necessarily old knowledge. Rather, "traditional Knowledge" is often dynamic and adaptive to changing culture patterns and wide range of external influences, including occupation of indigenous people's lands, market pressures over certain resources, re-settlement, etc. "Traditional Knowledge" often flows in oral forms and is not codified in writing or in systematised forms (i.e. books or

the terms "traditional knowledge" and "indigenous knowledge" could be interchangeable. The Convention on Biological Diversity (CBD) on the other hand, refers to indigenous people's knowledge, innovations and practices to highlight the intellectual effort of indigenous and local communities[2] as they relate to biodiversity conservation and sustainable use.

The term "traditional knowledge" is only one of various words used to address similar subject matter, namely, the intellectual effort and its results, generated by indigenous peoples and local communities, which has enabled them to adapt to and live in relative harmony with their natural environments throughout the centuries and contribute to modern society with innumerable products.[3]

---

databases). For some a key feature is its collective nature: knowledge is generated collectively in complex communal manners where no one individual can be recognized as a "creator" (this is not an issue over which no consensus exists although most people tend to agree on the collective nature of traditional knowledge). For further details on terminology see WIPO. Intellectual Needs and Property and "Traditional knowledge" Holders. WIPO Report on Fact Finding Missions on Intellectual Property and "traditional knowledge" (1998-99) Geneva, April, 2001.

2. Who owns "traditional knowledge" is possibly the hardest question which experts and indigenous communities themselves face when conseptualizing defensive or positive mechanisms to protect "traditional knowledge". Except for limited cases, particular and specific indigenous traditional knowledge is usually shared among a wide range of communities within countries and even among them. Determining who has the right to decide about "traditional knowledge" and what exactly does this right poses critical concerns which go beyond the scope of this paper, for discussion of this issue see: Vogel, Joseph. El Acrtel de la Biodiverside. Transformacion de los Conocimientos Tradicinales en Secretos Comerciales. SAN REM, Ecociencia, USAID. Quito, 2000.

3. For the purpose of this study and recognizing that there are differences between the concepts of "Indigenous communities" and "indigenous peoples" both will be used indifferently through the text. A commonly used term is that of the International Labor Convention 1969 Concerning Indigenous and Tribal People in Independent Countries which refers to "Indigenous Peoples" as "...peoples in independent countries whose social, culture and economic conditions distinguish them from other sections of the

The importance of "traditional knowledge" can be perceived by looking at simple facts: 85% to 90% of the basic livelihood need of the world's poor (more than half of the world's population, including indigenous and local communities) are based on direct use of biological resources (and related "traditional knowledge") for food, medicine, shelter, transport, etc.; over 1.4 billion poor farmers rely on farm saved seeds and local plants breeding techniques as their primary source of seed;[4] 57% of the top 150 brand name drugs prescribed during a six month period in 1993, contained at least one major active compound derived or patterned on compounds from biological diversity and of the 35 plant derived drugs included in the top 150 best selling drugs, 94% contained at least one compound with proven use in traditional medicinal practices by indigenous and local communities.[5] Areas of high concentration of biodiversity and the location of indigenous and local communities often coincide and evidence a pattern of close interrelation between nature, man and knowledge. Communities conserve, maintain, enhance and, in many instances, act as guardians of natural and biological resources.

On the other hand, the importance of traditional knowledge also reflects itself in other ways. Modern technologies, including biotechnology, which manipulate, use, adapt or transform biological resources often, use, either directly or indirectly indigenous knowledge at some point during product research and development process. Whether

---

national community, and whose status is regulated wholly or partially by their own customs or traditions or by special laws or regulations" [article 1(b)]. The CBD on the other hand refers to "indigenous and local communities", thus also including local communities (i.e. small farmers) which might not necessary be indigenous as would a native community in Amazon.

4. See: The Crubile II Group. Seeding Solutions. Volume 1: Policy options for genetic resources. People, Plants and Patents revised. IDRC, IPGRI, and Dag Hammarskjold Foundation, Italy, 2000, p. 1.
5. For further information see: Grifo, Francesca. The Origins of Prescription Drugs. In: Fracesca Grifo and Joshua Rosenthal (des.) Biodiversity and Human Health. Washington DC, Island Press, 1997.

using ethno botanical information found in scientific literature or databases or through direct consultation and interaction with indigenous peoples; traditional knowledge serves an important purpose as a valuable input directing and orienting research activities of universities and companies particularly during initial stages of research. Sectors which have benefited from these inputs include food, beverages, pharmaceuticals, chemicals, horticulture, agriculture, construction materials and cosmetics.[6]

2. PATENTS AND THE RELEVANCE OF PRIOR ART IN RELATION TO TRADITIONAL KNOWLEDGE

In broad terms, patents can be defined as exclusive rights granted for an invention—either a product or a process—that offers a new technical solution to a specific problem. A patent implies the grant of a "monopoly" to an inventor who has used his knowledge and skills to produce a product or process which is new, involves an inventive step and is capable of industrial application. This "monopoly" is limited in time and allows for the patent holder to exercise an exclusive right over the invention and benefit commercially from its exploitation.

The grant of a patent is conditioned upon the full public disclosure of the invention in order to enable others to improve on existing inventions and technology in general. Disclosure is key in order to help : (a) determine whether the claimed invention is in fact new (i.e. it does not form part of the state of the art) and not obvious to a person skilled in that particular technological field, and (b) to allow for other inventors to continue developing and improving technology based on the patented invention, thereby promoting the progress of science and technology. This is in principle, one of the most important counterweights for granting a patent holder exclusive rights in the marketplace. As a general rule, information which is in the public domain cannot be subject to patent claims. Disclosing traditional knowledge which forms

6. See: Ten Kate, Kerry and Larid, Sarah. The Commercial Use of Biodiversity. Access to Genetic Resources and Benefit Sharing. Earthscan Publications Ltd. London, 1999.

part of an invention and of the state of the art or prior art will promote the progress of science by creating an incentive for the maintenance of traditional knowledge systems. It will also create an incentive for indigenous peoples to continue traditional practices which have enabled them to maintain biodiversity *in situ*.[7] *This will elevate and promote the status of traditional knowledge. This will happen by traditional knowledge being widely and universally accepted within "western" or "modern" innovation protection systems and becoming a reference point within the regular operations of the international patent system.*

This is also a relevant aspect recognized by Article 8(j) of the CBD which calls upon parties to adopt measures to respect, preserve and maintain traditional knowledge, to promote its wider use (with the approval and involvement of indigenous peoples) and encourage the equitable sharing of benefits arising form the use of this knowledge.

3. TRADITIONAL KNOWLEDGE AS PRIOR ART

There has been considerable concern that patents have been granted for inventions which did not meet fundamental requirements for patentability, specifically in relation to the requirements of novelty and inventiveness, when compared to traditional knowledge from which these inventions might have been directly or indirectly derived.

Had this traditional knowledge been known to patent authorities—examiners in particular—at the time of review of patent application, it may have been considered as prior art and, subsequently, may have defeated the claims that the invention was new and involved an inventive step. This would have assisted in the prevention of "bio-piracy".

Prior art or the state of the art usually refers to the complete body of knowledge which is available to the public before a patent application is filed or, if a priority date is

7. See: CIEL. Comments on Improving Identification of Prior Art. Recommendations on Traditional Knowledge Relating to Biological Diversity Submitted to the United States Patents and Trademark Office, August 1999, p. 3.

claimed, before that priority date. Novelty is measured against the state of the art. The inventive step of an invention will be achieved when it is not obvious to a person skilled in the art, taking into account any matter which forms part of the state of the art. Patent authorities are responsible to ensure that these substantial requirements to patentability are met by the claimed invention before a patent is actually granted.[8]

In simple terms, the problem-relating prior art and traditional knowledge could be summarised as follows: although there is traditional knowledge being held and used by indigenous peoples (and researchers as well for their own academic and research purposes) and there are publications, databases, journals, periodicals and other means through which traditional knowledge is being disseminated and made public, traditional knowledge has rarely been recognized and considered as forming part of the state of the art for the purpose of the patent system in general. Seldom have patent examiners undertaken exhaustive searches and review of traditional knowledge sources, this has caused, especially in the United States, problem with patents such as those relating to Neem and Ayahuasca.

Reasons for this situation vary but include: not having access to traditional knowledge information in classified non-patent literature, not having adequate and effective search tools to retrieve this information and, in general, because this type of information is not systematically ordered and arranged to facilitate its use by patent examiners.[9] Curiously, the approach to this issue, particularly in the United States, is to grant patents and only when such patents are challenged, undertake comprehensive prior art searches. This situation is a major burden for indigenous communities which wish to nullify or invalidate patents over inventions or discoveries that have used or incorporated their traditional knowledge when (a) this knowledge already exists in the public domain, and (b) when this knowledge has been obtained without prior informed consent.

8. See Holyoak, Jon and Torremans, Paul. Intellectual Property Law. Second Edition. Butterworths, London, 1998 (Chapter 3, section B).
9. See document WIPO/GRTKF/OC/2/6, paragraph 5.

1. Definitions of Prior Art and Search Practices in the US, Japan and under the European Patent Convention

Sub-sections 102(a) and (b) of the US Patent Act (35 U.S.C.) establish that a patent will not be granted if the invention was patented or described in a printed publication in the US or a foreign country, either before the sate of the claimed invention or more than a year before the date of the patent application. A patent shall not be granted also if the invention was known or used by others in the foreign country. Unpublished or Un-patented knowledge or use in a foreign country is not relevant to patentability under the sub-section.

Sub-section 102(f) is also relevant in that it determines that a patent will not be awarded when the applicant did not invent the actual subject matter to be patented. In this regard, any information—including traditional knowledge—published or unpublished, in the US or abroad, demonstrating that the applicant is not the actual inventor can be material to patentability. Therefore, patent claims that merely duplicate processes known to indigenous communities should he rejected.[10]

According to US law, patent authorities (in this case the US Patent and Trademark Office—USPTO) should carry out a thorough investigation of available prior art relating to the subject mater. The key consideration is to determine whether information is available or not. Prior art will be available when an examiner can access this information through written texts, databases, published herbarium specimens (in the case of plant patents) or other sources, or when it is provided by the applicant as part of his disclosure obligation.[11]

Recent cases of biopiracy (including the Turmeric and Ayahuasca cases) demonstrate the need for patent examiners in the United States to consistently access and adequately evaluate prior art to ensure patents are not awarded in cases

10. See CIEL. Comments on Improving Identification of Prior Art: Recommendations on Traditional Knowledge Relating to Biodiversity Submitted to the United States and Trade Office. August 2, 1999.
11. See *Ibid.*, p. 4.

where the subject matter is broader than what was actually invented.

Examiners should also review all known databases and registers of traditional knowledge in order to ensure that patents actually involve an inventive step and should additionally integrate existing rules, practices and guidelines governing international searches (i.e. PCT) into routine examination procedures.

In order to address these issues and avoid patenting of traditional knowledge, the USPTO has suggested the need to create more easily accessible non-patent literature database that deal with traditional knowledge. Traditional knowledge could, in this way, be documented, captured electronically and placed under appropriate classification systems in order for it to be more easily searched and retrieved by patent examiners. On the other hand, Section 29 of the Japanese Patent Law provides that prior art entails: (a) inventions which were publicly known; (b) inventions which were publicly worked; and (c) inventions which were described in a distributed publication or made available to the public through telecommunication lines in Japan or elsewhere, prior to the filing date or priority date.

Complementary to the above criteria, the Japanese *Operational Guidelines on Treatment of Technical Information Disclosed on the Internet as Prior Art (December, 1999)*, offer detailed guidance as to the treatment as prior art of inventions which became available to the general public through communication lines prior to the filing of the patent application. These "telecommunication lines", as defined, would include websites and on line databases of traditional knowledge. Availability of the information—even if not effectively accessed—is therefore important. As long as access is not restricted to the websites or databases (even if a password or non-discriminating procedure is required), these will be considered available to the general public and therefore, be considered to contain information which could be considered prior art.[12] The same principles would obviously apply to written documentation.

12. See WIPO/GRTKF/Inter-governmental Committee/2/6, paragraphs 56-59.

In the case of Europe, Article 54(2) of the EPC defines prior art (the state of the art) as comprising "*. . . everything made available to the public by means of a written or oral description, by use, or in any other way, before the filing of the European patent application*". EPC jurisprudence has made it clear that the issue is not so much whether the general public are aware of the existence of the information but, rather, that the information is simply available and accessible to anyone at any given time (before the application is filed). This is particularly important with regards to traditional knowledge and information sources of which the general public might not be readily aware,[13]

> Patent searches in the European Patent Office (EPO), seek to discover the state of the art or prior art which is relevant for the purpose of determining whether an invention to which the patent application relates is new and involves an inventive step. This is basically a documentary search. The documentation includes patent documents, complemented by articles, periodicals and other non-patent literature. The search will be as comprehensive and exhaustive as possible, with limitations imposed by economic considerations. As an International Searching Authority under the PCT system, the EPO will carry out the search based on documentation specified in PCT Regulations.[14]

Due to economic considerations, a search examiner will use his discretion to end his search when the probability of discovering further relevant prior art becomes very low in relation to the effort needed. The search will also be stopped when the documents found clearly demonstrate a lack of novelty in the subject matter of the claimed invention and its elaboration in the description would not amount to an inventive step.[15]

13. See *Ibid.*, paragraphs 53-54.
14. See: Guidelines for Examination in the European Patent Office. EPO, June 2000, p. 2.
15. See *Ibid.*, p. 17.

2. The Patent Cooperation Treaty (PTC): Prior Art Definition and Disclosure Requirements[16]

The PCT was concluded in Washington D.C. in 1970 and to date there are over 100 countries which have ratified the Agreement. The PCT is only an international system for processing patent applications and formal granting of patents remains under national or regional jurisdiction.

The PCT process consists of two phases: an international phase and a national phase. The international phase is based upon: an international application, an international search, an international publication and international preliminary examination. The national phase is made up of different procedures which an applicant needs to carry out with the designated office once the international phase is over.

It is the international phase procedures and institutional capacities of searching authorities, which make PCT an important instrument with which to promote alternatives for considering traditional knowledge either during the International Search or as part of an International preliminary Examination.

Article 15(1) and (2) of the PCT establish that international applications will be subject to an international search. This search aims at discovering relevant prior art

16. The PCT is particularly relevant to the traditional knowledge and prior art discussions because of the international nature of its prior art searching procedures and the advantages it offers. The international search—through an International Searching Authority—is carried out by national offices of Australia, Austria, China, Japan, the Republic of Korea, Russian Federation, Sweden, the US and the European Patent Office. High Quality, although not binding, International Search Reports and International Preliminary Examinations provide patent applicants with an additional and considerable degree of certainty with regards to the patentability of their inventions, therefore its novelty, inventiveness and industrial application. Institutional capacities, human resources and financial resources available in these offices make them the ideal to ensure comprehensive and rigorous patent searches. For further details on the advantages of the PCT see: WIPO. Basic Facts about the Patent Cooperation Treaty. The Worldwide system for simplified multiple filing of patent applications, WIPO, April 2002.

which, for the purposes of the PCT is defined by Rule 33.1 of the PCT Regulations as ". . . everything which has been made available to the public anywhere in the world by means of written disclosure (including drawing and other illustrations) and which is capable of being of assistance in determining that the claimed invention is or is not new and that it does not involve an inventive step (i.e. that it is or is not obvious), provided that the making available to the public occurred prior to the international filing date.[17]

It seems clear that oral disclosure, use, exhibition or other means of disclosure will only be considered relevant during an international search if they are substantiated by *written* disclosure. Indeed, as important (and common) as oral traditions might be among indigenous communities, there are practical aspects of patent searching procedures which would make it necessary to evidence and substantiate traditional knowledge and practices in some written form.

The international search[18] will cover all technical fields, which may contain material pertinent to the invention and involve subject matter that is usually recognized as equivalent to the subject matter of the claimed invention for all or certain of its features. The International Searching Authority will "...endeavor to discover as much of the relevant prior art as its facilities permit, and shall, in any case, consult the documentation specified in the Regulation.[19] Furthermore, the international search ". . . in so far as possible and reasonable, will cover entire subject matter to which the claims are directed or to which they might be reasonably be expected to be directed after they have been amended".[20] An International Searching Authority should therefore endeavor to discover as much of the relevant prior art as its facilities permit. In any

17. See: Rule 33.1 (a) Regulations Under the PCT.
18. The International Search Report contains: citation of the documents considered relevant, classification of the subject matter (according to the International Patent Classification), an indication of the fields which have been searched and any electronic database searched. Citations of particular relevance must be especially indicated.
19. See: Article 15(4) PCT.
20. See Rule 33.3(b) : Regulations under the PCT.

case, the authority must consult the so-called minimum documentation.[21]

The current minimum documentation list was agreed upon during the Fourth Plenary Session of the *Standing Committee on Information Technology* (SCIT) (December 6-10, 1999) and came into effect in January 2000. As a means to incorporate traditional knowledge into international searches, one option could be that periodicals, newsletters, gazettes and other publications which document traditional knowledge be integrated into the minimum documentation list.

Incorporating traditional knowledge sources in the *Journal of Patent Associated Literature* (JOPAL), a centralized database of bibliographic data used to aid patent offices in search of technical and scientific non-patent literature, could also play an important role in ensuring comprehensive prior art searches with regards to traditional knowledge.

The Inter-governmental committee on Intellectual Property and Genetic Resources, Traditional Knowledge and Folklore (the "inter-governmental Committee")[22] under Tusk B.3, is assessing how best to ensure that the International Searching Authority can carry out international searches and discover pertinent

21. Minimum documentation comprises: Patent documents issued by France after 1919; by Germany from 1920 to 1045 and by the Federal Republic of Germany since 1945; by Japan (for International Searching Authorities other than the Japan Patent Office) only those documents for which English abstracts are available; by the former Soviet Union and now the Russian Federation (for International Searching Authorities other than the Russian Patent Office) only those documents for which English abstracts are available; by Switzerland (except documents in Italian); by the United Kingdom; by the United States of America; by the African Intellectual Property Organisation; by the European Patent Office and by the Eurasian Patent Office. It also includes published international PCT applications and from various sources including periodicals. If an International Searching Authority has more documents available it is obliged to consult them to the extent permitted by its facilities. See: Chapter VII, volume I of the PCT Applicants Guide.
22. The Inter-governmental Committee was established by the WIPO General Assembly at its Twenty-sixth Session held in Geneva form September 26 to October 3, 2000, see document: WO/GA/26/6 at http://www.wipo.int.

traditional knowledge when it constitutes prior art in relation to the invention. At present, the International Search Guidelines of the PCT and overall practices of designated searching authorities do not include a specific requirement for the review of traditional knowledge information or data.

PCT also offers, upon demand of the applicant, an *International Preliminary Examination.*[23] The preliminary examination which is carried out by an *International Preliminary Examining Authority*[24] is intended to provide a confidential non-binding report regarding novelty, inventiveness and industrial applicability. This report does not however address issues of patentability under any specific existing law or regulation. It merely states whether the claims appear to comply with the criteria of novelty, inventiveness and industrial application as defined in the PCT. Although there are no uniform approaches to these criteria in national laws, their application under the PCT during the international phase gives the applicant a good idea of the likely results during the national phase.

Finally, with regards to non-written disclosures, the PCT provides that "*. . . in cases where the making available to the public occurred by means of an oral disclosure use exhibition or other non-written means (non-written disclosure) before the relevant date as defined in Rule 64.1(b) and the date of such non-written disclosure is indicated in a written disclosure which has been made available to the public on a date which is the same as, or later than, the relevant date, the non-written disclosure shall not be considered part of the prior art for the purpose of article 33(2) and (3). Nevertheless, the international preliminary examination report shall call attention to such non-written disclosure in the manner provided for in Rule 70g*".

3. The Current Discussion in WIPO on Traditional Knowledge as Prior Art

During the first session of the Inter-governmental Committee[25] held from April 30 to May 3, 2001, Member

23. See: Article 31(1) of the PCT.
24. These are generally the same as International Searching Authorities.
25. See: WIPO/GA/26/6 at http://www.wipo.int

States agreed upon an agenda of work and items to be prioritized by the Inter-governmental Committee. Under Agenda Item 5.2 (Protection of Traditional Knowledge) a series of tasks were proposed; Tasks B.1 to B.4. In terms of Task B.3[26] Member States expressed their wish to consider and examine existing criteria and the need for possible new criteria to allow for more effective integration of traditional knowledge documentation into searchable prior art.[27]

At its Second Session, held on December 10-14, 2001, the Intergovernmental Committee considered the *Progress Report on the Status of Traditional Knowledge as Prior Art*[28] and debated extensively on implementation of Task B.3. Five overall activities were considered in order to implement Task B.3. These included: compiling an inventory of existing traditional knowledge periodicals in order to discuss whether they might be considered by the PCT International Searching Authorities as part of their minimum documentation requirements (Possible Activity 1): as a result of possible activity 1, assess whether prioritized periodicals might be incorporated into JOPAL project (Possible Activity 2); discuss possible recommendations to consider traditional knowledge as prior art in amendments to guidelines for patent searches and examinations (Possible Activity 3); assess the feasibility of the electronic exchange of public domain traditional knowledge documentation data, including through the creation of a database and digital library (Possible Activity 4); examine applicability of existing intellectual property documentation standards to traditional knowledge-related subject mater (Possible Activity 5); and discuss means of assisting indigenous peoples and traditional knowledge documentation initiatives (Possible Activity 6).

One key issue is how to ensure prior art searches carried out by patent authorities take adequate consideration of traditional knowledge. Even though throughout the world there is a large amount of documented traditional knowledge, there are current limitations as to how patent procedure can

26. See: WIPO/GRTKF/IC/1/3.
27. See: WIPO/GRTKF/IC/2/6.
28. WIPO/GRTKF/IC/2/6.

include broader and more comprehensive searches for prior art and thereby prevent misappropriation of traditional knowledge. These limitations however, seem to stem from regular practices rather than from fundamental difficulties (or even legal restrictions) which patent authorities face.

Additionally, the analysis would also have to extend to how traditional knowledge might be positively protected.[29] It is not enough to focus on defensive protection although it can be supported as an initial step towards overall protection of traditional knowledge.[30]

Addressing these concerns will necessarily require: (a) assessing how public domain information relating to traditional knowledge can be made available for patent offices,[31] (b) allowing patent offices to formally integrate the

29. Negative or preventive protection of traditional knowledge refers to the use of mechanisms to impede traditional knowledge from being misappropriated. For example, the prior art search (for traditional knowledge) during patent procedures and ensuring non-obviousness of an invention are two ways through which negative protection can be ensured. It is a preventive measure and a reaction to an action (filing of a patent). Positive protection refers to mechanisms which ensure rights are actually provided and conferred to indigenous peoples with regards to their traditional knowledge.
30. For a review of policy and legal advances in regimes for the protection of traditional knowledge in Suriname, Guyana, Brazil, Colombia, Venezuela, Ecuador, Peru and Bolivia see: Ruiz, Manuel. Protection *sui generis* de economientos indigenous en la Anazonia. Corporation Andina de Fomento, Parlamento Andino y Socieded Peruna de Derecho Ambiental. Lima, 2002.
31. Discussions are still ongoing as circumstances where traditional knowledge can be or not be considered as being in the public domain. For example, it is not the same to have traditional knowledge recorded and codified in a widely available database as to have traditional knowledge available within indigenous peoples' contexts alone (i.e. available within a few organized communities). The question to ask is whether it could be argued that in the latter case, traditional knowledge is in fact in the public domain. In any case it should be assumed that the information and data which could eventually be incorporated into publicly available database will be information and data, which is at least accessible, and, therefore, in the public domain. For further discussion see: WIPO/GRTKF/Inter-governmental Committee/2/6.

analysis of this information into their procedures for examining and granting patents, and (c) developing appropriate information systems (including databases) on traditional knowledge. The development of such information systems would have to take into account whether centralized information systems are needed or whether decentralized but inter-connected systems might be a better option. Most importantly, due consideration would have to be given to the impact which codifying Traditional knowledge might have on traditional knowledge cultures and livelihoods.[32]

The following few paragraphs describe past and present work within WIPO bodies in relation to this issue of traditional knowledge and prior art debates.

WIPO Standing Committee on Information Technology (SCIT)

During its Third Plenary Session, (June 14-15, 1999), the SCIT adopted a Strategic Information Technology Plan into the 21st Century which includes references to the need to create traditional knowledge databases for traditional knowledge in the public domain. At its Fourth Plenary Session (December 6-10, 1999 the SCIT considered an Approach Paper for Establishing Traditional Knowledge Digital Libraries (TKDL) which, in turn, is part of WIPO Intellectual Property Digital

32. Larid, Alexaides, Bannister and Posey argue that "...knowledge within communities is not equally distributed; rather it is distributed and exchanged according to particular norms and criteria, all of which may be disrupted by the publication process". Furthermore, they also suggest that due to the vary complex ways in which knowledge is generated and flows within indigenous communities "...removal or transfer of information from the group through publication can threaten internal and external stability". Knowledge will be misrepresented, weakened and misused. Finally, these authors recognize that there is an international trend—probably fuelled in part by the CBD—towards greater consultation with groups regarding publication of their knowledge. See: Larid, S., Alexaides, M. Bannister, K. Posey, D. Publication of Biodiversity Reaserch Results and the Flow of Knowledge. In: Larid, Sarah (ed). 2002. *Biodiversity and Traditional Knowledge. Equitable Partnerships in Practice.* WWF, RBGKew and UNESCO. EARthscan Publications Ltd. London, p. 82.

Libraries (IPDL). The IPDL initiative seeks to identify and develop data exchange standards to be used by WIPO Member States Offices and the IPDL systems implemented by the International Bureau and to provide maximum level of integrated access to WIPO IP data collections. Although the SCIT decided not to pursue the TKDL within its Program, it did recognize the need to consider the exchange of traditional knowledge within the overall approach of WIPO to the issue of traditional knowledge.[33]

WIPO Committee of Experts of the Special Union for International Patent Classification Union (IPC Union)

At the Thirtieth Session, the Committee of Experts of the IPC Union (February, 2002), agreed that a Task Force (made up of representatives for China, India, Japan, United States and the European Patent Office) be created in order to study the Traditional Knowledge Resources Classification (TKRC) of the TKDL as presented by India and assess its information aspects and relation to the IPC. The IPC Committee noted that: (a) the most efficient way of developing classification tools for traditional knowledge would be their integration into the IPC, (b) the IPC could be used for classifying non-patent, traditional knowledge information, (c) work of the Task Force should be carried out with a view of an IPC revision proposal, and (d) the Task Force should look at ways in which a revised IPC could be linked to traditional knowledge classifications.[34]

WIPO Standing Committee on the Law Patents (SCP)

The SCP is at present discussing the definition of "prior art" in the context of the development of the draft *Substantive Patent Law Treaty (SPLT)*. As part of its information gathering activities, the SCP has received a series of responses from countries with regard to the prior art effect on patentability of information disclosed on the Internet. As a general rule, some national patent authorities limit the use of the Internet for the purpose of prior art searches to websites and database of high

33. For further information on this see documents: SCIT/3/2 item 7.2; SCIT/4/2 Annex II; SCIT/4/8.
34. For details see: WIPO/GRTKF/IGC/3/5.

credibility. Others categorize websites according to their credibility.

One key problem regarding websites is timing and contents of Internet databases and overall information. Suggestions of a "certification service" to certify timing of disclosed and content of websites received mixed reactions. Many countries, however, expressed their concerns regarding the cost and effectiveness of such a mechanism and there is probably a considerable need to assess the feasibility and desirability of such a certification scheme.[35]

During the Seventh Session of the SCP (May 6-10, 2002) the draft Article 8 of the SPLT on the definition of prior art was discussed. The draft provisions basically provide that prior art refers to any information made available to the public *anywhere* in the world in any form as prescribed in the Regulations, before the relevant claim. Under Rule 8 of the draft Regulations it is provided that information made available to the public in any form, such as written from, by oral communication, by display, or through use, shall qualify as prior art under Article 8(1).

The Inter-governmental Committee

The Inter-governmental Committee was established in the year 2000 after extensive discussion within WIPO and its Member States on intellectual property and genetic resources issues. The Inter-governmental Committee was established to provide a forum for discussion among Member States on intellectual property issues that arise in the context of: (a) access to genetic resources and benefit sharing, (b) protection of traditional knowledge, and (c) protection of expressions of folklore. These are cross-cutting issues which affect conventional intellectual property ranches but do not fit into existing bodies such as the SCP or the SCIT. Work within the Inter-governmental Committee was expected to complement and be consistent with advances in the CBD

35. Information on the Internet, particularly with regards to traditional knowledge, presents a challenge regarding when exactly the information was incorporated into the Internet. This relates to the issue of filling and priority dates of a patent application.

process and the Commission on Genetic Resources for Food and Agriculture (CGRFA) of the Food and Agriculture Organization (FAO).

During its Third Session (June 13-21, 2002) the Intergovernmental Committee discussed among other issues, the inventory of traditional knowledge-related periodicals, existing intellectual property protection of traditional knowledge and elements of a *sui generis* system for the protection of traditional knowledge.

4. OTHER FORUMS WORKING ON TRADITIONAL KNOWLEDGE

There are numerous other forums and institutions working on different aspects of traditional knowledge. Some of the main forums and institutions that deal with the issue of traditional knowledge, prior art and databases include, the CBD, the World Health Organisation (WHO) and the WTO in its Committee on Trade and Environment (CTE) and in the TRIPS Council.

The Convention on Biological Diversity. Within the work of the Ad Hoc Working Group on Article 8(j) and Related Provisions, activities have been proposed to develop guidelines and standards to prevent misappropriation of traditional knowledge in general. The Fifth Conference of the Parties (COP) called upon Parties to support the development of national registers of traditional knowledge, Innovations and practices.[36] The Panel of Experts on Access to Genetic Resources also agreed that developing registers could assist in identifying and promoting recognition of traditional knowledge as prior art.[37]

World Health Organisation: The WHO coordinates a Traditional Medicine Team set-up to support countries in developing national strategies on traditional Medicine and upgrading the knowledge of traditional medicine practitioners. During an inter-regional Workshop on Intellectual Property Rights in the Context of Traditional Medicine (Bangkok,

36. See Decision V/16 of COP V, Annex IV.
37. See document UNEP/CBD/COP/5/8 paragraphs 136-38.

December, 2000) it was recommended that traditional knowledge in the public domain should be documented in the form of digital libraries and exchanged and disseminated through mechanisms related to intellectual property rights. Work in this regard should be coordinated with WIPO.[38]

WTO's Committee on Trade and the Environment and the TRIPs Council : Work and discussions have progressed mainly in the area traditional knowledge and database, and how these might serve as defensive mechanisms against "bio-piracy". Under the review of Article 27.3(b) of the TRIPs Agreement one proposal is that features and main characteristics of an international database on traditional knowledge could include: the need for this database to be international in scope; the need for the database to act as a gateway to existing regional and national databases (not a centralized database *per se*); the need for this mechanism to be administrated by WIPO.[39]

Still other forums and institutions working on different aspects of traditional knowledge and indigenous and local peoples in general include: the World Bank, the United Nations Conference on Trade and Environment (UNCTAD), the Andean Community of Nations, the Inter-American Development Bank and the African Union, to name a few.

5. KEY ISSUES AND OPTIONS TO CONSIDER IN DEVELOPING MECHANISMS UNDER THE PATENT SYSTEM TO IMPEDE OR LIMIT MISAPPROPRIATION OF TRADITIONAL KNOWLEDGE

It is useful to highlight some basic considerations regarding traditional knowledge, prior art, disclosure and patentability discussion in order to propose practical recommendations to address the problems which the linkages between these elements bring about. Some of the main considerations include the fact that:

38. See http://www.who.org
39. See document IP/C/W/284, paragraph 17

- there is abundant information on codified traditional knowledge in existing publications, databases, periodicals, journals, etc.,
- much of this information could be considered to be the public domain,
- some of this information has been collected without prior informed consent form indigenous and local communities,
- most of this information is not organized nor classified in a systematic manner and is only exceptionally used by the patent system in order to evaluate prior art and determine novelty and inventiveness; more often, it has been used to challenge patents already grated,
- using databases for protecting defensively and positively traditional knowledge is not mutually exclusive,
- some indigenous peoples are using databases to document and protect their rights, for example, the Tulatip tribes in the United States,[40]
- incorporating traditional knowledge into systematic and organized databases,[41] even when already in the public domain, raises questions regarding the impact of these organizational measures on indigenous peoples' cultures and also calls for an assessment of the potential effects of this organizational system on positive protection of traditional knowledge,[42] and

40. See, Tulatip Natural Resources. Culture Stories. ICONS CD ROM, 2002.
41. Another issue for consideration is the possibility of developing registers (databases) with differentiated levels of accessibility, depending on the purpose of accessing the pertinent information. This could enable the register to serve a two tier purpose on one hand it can act as a defensive protection measure but also have a positive protection feature in the case of certain traditional knowledge which is kept under greater restrictions. For further discussion see: WIPO/GRTKF/Inter-governmental Committee/3/6, paragraph 55.
42. A good example here might be the International Cooperative Biodiversity Group project in Peru. Indigenous communities managed to negotiate contractual conditions for the use of their

- although negative or defensive protection—preventing bio-piracy through patents—goes one step forward in ensuring the patent system operates appropriately, it is only a measure out of a series of potentially useful approaches to ensure protection of traditional knowledge which is, ultimately, the main challenge.

A. Disclosure Requirements

As a general rule, patent applicants should disclose to the patent authority all information known to be material to patentability. Such information could include description of traditional knowledge utilized in the invention.

For this purpose, patent authorities could require that applicants:

- Conduct their own prior art searches of traditional knowledge and include that information in the application,
- Disclose source country (or traditional knowledge holder communities), and
- Ensure that use of traditional knowledge complies with national laws[43] (i.e. on access to and use of

knowledge which was in the public domain, although limited to the communities which shared this knowledge. Knowledge had not flowed outside their communities. If this knowledge had been recorded and organized in a functional, publicly available database it would have been harder if not impossible for communities to argue the need to negotiate over now codified and recorded traditional knowledge. The fact that knowledge is not recorded nor codified (even if in the public domain) provides indigenous communities with an opportunity to negotiate over its use. For an analysis of this case see: Tobin, B. Chapter 9. *Biodiversity and Traditional Knowledge. Equitable Partnerships in Practice*. WWF, RBGKew and UNESCO. Earthscan Publications Ltd. London, pp. 287-309.

43. An example is provided by Decision 486 of the Andean Community of Nations on Common Regime on Industrial Property. As part of the initial patent application procedure, the patent examiner, when provided with evidence that traditional knowledge or genetic resources of which the five Member States of the Andean

genetic resources and traditional knowledge)[44] and international principles regarding prior informed consent and benefit sharing under the CBD.[45]

B. Search Procedures

As has already been pointed out, many of the shortcoming and limitation of the patent system to deal with

---

Community of Nations are source countries or countries of origin respectively, has the right to require from the applicant evidence that traditional knowledge or resources used in his invention have been legally obtained. This mechanism leaves a degree of discretion to the examiner in order to demand these in cases where sufficient evidence is at hand to suggest traditional knowledge has been utilized. This is not considered a patentibility requirement but a formal procedural condition as part of the administrative application process. For further analysis of this particular mechanism and regime see respectively: Pires de Carvalho, Nuno. Requiring Disclosure of the Origin of Genetic Resources and Prior Informed Consent in Patent Application Without Infringing the TRIPs Agreement: The Problem and the Solution. In: *Washington University Journal of Law and Policy*. Vol. 2, 2000 and Ruiz, Manuel. Analisis de la Decision 486 de Resources Geneticos y Conocimientors Tradicionales. Documento preparado para la Corporacion Andina de Fomento (version en brrador). Lima, 2002.

44. Countries such as Panama, Costa Rica, Brazil and the Andean Community of Nations (Venezuela, Colombia, Ecuador, Peru and Bolivia) have laws in place which establish basic requirements to access and use traditional knowledge. These laws however, generally refer to cases where knowledge is sought directly, *in situ*, for indigenous communities. They do not address the issue of knowledge kept in publicly available databases or in the public domain in general.

45. International law should, generally, form a coherent system of principles and norms which complement each other or, at least, do not conflict among each other. In this sense, complying with this requirements enables the patent system to support the realization of the CBD objectives, particularly with regards to benefit sharing. Relevant articles linking the CBD to the intellectual property regime include:

    Article 8(j) : Each Contracting Party shall as far as possible and appropriate : Subjects to its national legislation, respect, preserve and maintain knowledge, innovations and practices of indigenous and local communities embodying traditional lifestyles relevant for

misappropriation stem from the fact that procedures for actually examining patent applications have, in broad terms, not been designed to consider traditional knowledge in the search of prior art even if in principle there is no reason why this should not be so.

In this regard, possible options to ensure traditional knowledge is not misappropriated through the patent system could include:

- Ensuring that the patent application examination procedure (at the national level and particularly with regards to PCT) reviews and takes into account all accessible and available information contained in databases (particularly through the World Wide Web), publications and other sources of traditional knowledge.[46]

---

the conservation and sustainable use of biological diversity and promote their wider application with the approval and involvement of the holders of such knowledge, innovations and practices and encourage the equitable sharing of benefits arising from the utilization of such knowledge, innovations and practices.

Article 10(c) : Each Contracting Party shall as far as possible : Protect and encourage customary use of biological resources in accordance with traditional practices that are compatible with conservation and sustainable use requirements.

Article 16(5): The Contracting Parties, recognizing that patent and other intellectual property rights may have an influence on the implementation of this Convention, shall cooperate in this regard subject to national legislation and international.

46. Implementation of the CBD in the area of conserving, maintaining and promoting wider application of traditional knowledge (article 8(j)) is paving the way for the development of mechanisms and instruments devised in order to confer positive and defensive protection of traditional knowledge. Most of these are related to the development of registers of traditional knowledge (databases). As precise and comprehensive prior art searches in the fields of traditional knowledge. The CBD Clearing House Mechanism should become an alternative to provide a single and centralized entry point to worldwide databases on traditional knowledge.

C. The Relationship between the TRIPS Agreement and the CBD

Ways need to be devised to ensure that the TRIPs Agreement and the CBD are mutually supportive, even if their objectives point to different overall goals. With regards to patents in particulars, the TRIPs Agreement should be amended to, at the very least, ensure that when patents are granted over biologically derived inventions which might incorporate traditional knowledge, the granting procedures require applicants to provide evidence showing that:

- The materials were accessed legally,[47]
- Traditional knowledge when, and if used, was obtained, used or incorporated into the invention with the consent of the corresponding knowledge holders,[48] and
- There exist mutually agreed terms for benefit sharing.

In this regard, article 29.1 of the TRIPs Agreement, which provides that the applicant ". . . shall disclose the invention in

---

47. This requirement was in fact first put into practice as part of the Peruvian regulation of plant breeders' rights whereas applicant is required to provide legal evidence of the origin of genetic material contained in the plant variety and of the knowledge (including traditional knowledge) which was used in the variety (Supreme Decree 008-96-INDECOPI, 1996). Subsequently, Decision 391 of the Andean community on a Common Regime on Access to Genetic Resources also include this same requirement as does the recent Decision 486 on a Common Regime on Industrial Property (2001). Countries like Brazil, Costa Rica, Denmark, India and others are also including these types of provisions into their access laws or intellectual property regulations.
48. If in the case of the Budapest Treaty on the International Recognition of the Deposit of Micro-organisms, disclosure of biotechnological invention—and, furthermore, this does not run counter to the TRIPs Agreement nor article 29.1, it is possible to argue that the additional requirements suggested (i.e. disclosure of origin of the material and prior informed consent) could also be part of an adequate and full disclosure of the invention.

a manner sufficiently clear and complete for the invention to be carried out by a person skilled in the art and may require the applicant to indicate the best mode for carrying out the invention known to the inventor. . ." could be amended to include these requirements as part of the patent application procedure and especially the disclosure of the origin of the genetic resources and traditional knowledge.

D. Access to Genetic Resources (Traditional Knowledge) and Patent Authorities

Most biodiversity rich countries in the world have either developed or will soon have on place national legislation regulating access to genetic resources and, in some cases, provisions regulating access to and use of traditional knowledge. Whereas the problems presented above will be dealt with in areas where patents and biotechnology are mostly involved it is important that:

- National (and international) patent authorities maintain close communication and exchanging information regarding specific instances where genetic resources have been accessed and traditional knowledge is being used for commercial or industrial purposes, and (b) applications which might involve use of these resources and knowledge.[49]

E. Review of the Patent Classification System

Due to regular and internalized practices of national and

49. What exactly is the nature of these linkages remains to be discussed. One example is provided by the Complementary Disposition of Decision 391 of the Andean Community on a Common Regime on Access to Genetic Resources which establishes that "... National (Access) Authorities and National Authorities of Intellectual Property will establish information exchange systems regarding access to genetic resources contracts and intellectual property rights granted". This could not only help in initiating legal actions if resources have been obtained illegally but also assist searches during the patent application procedure in general.

international authorities in the use of the International Patent Classification system:

- A review of or amendment to the IPC prove extremely useful in assisting patent examination authorities with a widely utilized tool for the patent examination process.

F. Additional Minimum Documentation

Due to the importance of indigenous knowledge and its use in research and development processes in a series of industries and its incorporation into patents:

- The minimum documentation list of the PCT system should include traditional knowledge-related materials (books, gazettes, periodicals and databases).

In addition, JOPAL could also add traditional knowledge documentation sources into its bibliographic references.

G. Prior Informed Consent and Awareness Raising

Although there is an increased level of participation of indigenous people representatives in international forums (including the Inter-governmental Committee) and an awareness raising process has in practice begun on these issues, it could prove useful:

- For WIPO to support national consultative process where indigenous communities are informed and asked the possibility of codifying, centralizing or simply systematizing traditional knowledge in databases.

This process could help—to a certain extent and certainly not fully—to legitimize certain efforts and initiatives which are being undertaken to create traditional knowledge databases at the national and international level. Extreme care should be taken in order to ensure that traditional knowledge recorded is traditional knowledge which is in the public domain.[50]

H. Operations of Databases

When developing and designing databases for prior art purposes (either at the local, national or international level), the following considerations should be taken into account:

- All information collected, even if already in the public domain, should, as far as possible, be collected by or with the full informed consent of communities,
- The database could have levels of confidentially and restricted access depending on user of information and purposes of use,
- Representatives of indigenous and local communities should be involved in managing database,
- Rather than designing mega databases, countries should develop official databases which link up—through a clearing house—to an international database which could be the gateway for patent examining authorities worldwide,
- The structure of databases, organization of information, timing, certification, language used should be standardized,
- Information which is clearly not in the public domain (i.e. remains in oral form and has not left the ambit of specific indigenous communities or groups) should not be recorded,
- Inclusion of traditional knowledge in databases should not, as far as legally and practically possible, strict the rights which indigenous peoples might have over the information, and

50. This is particularly relevant activity in the light of experiences where traditional knowledge databases have been developed and widely made known to the public but where there have also been claims from indigenous communities themselves in the sense that the information contained in these database was not obtained with the full informed consent of communities.

- No intellectual property rights should be claimed over these national or international databases.

Databases could be an important tool in as they can be utilized in a practical and efficient manner, by communities and, especially, by patent searching authorities. Although communities, countries, institutions and even regions may be developing their own particular databases, according to specific realities and unique sets of criteria and considerations, there needs to be some degree of standardization if this mechanism is to be effective at the international level. However, this leads to a critical issue which will have to be further discussed with communities themselves: consolidating a tool which, in essence, will make traditional knowledge much more easily and readily accessible throughout the world for a wide ranging set of possible uses.

Traditional knowledge which is in the public domain—especially when the knowledge has surpassed the physical and geographical boundaries of communities—could be hard, but not impossible to protect in positive terms. However, focusing all efforts in positively protecting this type of knowledge will almost surely imply very high transaction costs which make the effort costly and even ineffective. It might be useful to suggest appealing to "good corporate practices" or institutional codes of conduct which, recognizing the vulnerability of traditional knowledge has left communities often without them knowing so or not being fully informed. The draft regulation in Peru, for example, incorporates this approach and seeks to create an incentive so that a potential user of traditional knowledge in the public domain, at least considers the possibility of negotiating with communities over this knowledge.

6

PVPFR Act—A Legislation Creating Multiple Ownership Rights

1. STAKEHOLDERS' INTERESTS AND THE NEW REGIME

The main feature of the Act is the provision to claim IPRs over varieties through a system of registration. The Act allows four types of varieties to be registered reflecting the interests of actors: New Variety, Extant Variety, Essentially Derived Variety and Farmers' Variety. The definition, criteria and term of protection of each of these varieties as elaborated in the Act are outlined in Table 6.1.

The four types of varieties correspond with the interests of specific actors as illustrated and described in further detail below (*Note*: legally any actor can apply for any type of variety. This represents only the type of protection that each actor could most likely benefit form):

TABLE 6.1

Varieties Protect Able under India's PVPFR Act

Type	*Section*	*Definition*	*Criteria*	*Right Granted*	*Duration*
(1)	*(2)*	*(3)*	*(4)*	*(5)*	*(6)*
New Variety	S2(za)	'Variety' means a plant grouping except microorganism defined by certain characteristics under the Act. It is new if it meets specified criteria.	Novelty Distinctness Uniformity Stability	Exclusive right for the breeder to produce, sell, market, distribute, import or export the variety.	Initially 9 years renewable up to total of 18 years for trees and vines. Initially 6 years renewable up to total of 15 for other crops.
Extant Variety	S2(j)	A variety available in India which is notified under Section 5 of the Seeds Act, 1966; or a farmers' variety; or a variety about which there is common knowledge; or any other variety which is in the public domain.	Distinctness Uniformity Stability as specified under the regulations.	Exclusive right to produce, sell, market, distribute, import or export the variety if claimed by the breeder and in cases where not claimed by breeder, the Central Government or State Government shall have the right.	15 years from the date of notification of that variety by the Central Government under Section 5 of the Seeds Act, 1966.

(Contd.)

TABLE 6.1 (Contd.)

(1)	(2)	(3)	(4)	(5)	(6)
Farmers' Variety	S2(l)	A variety which has been traditionally cultivated and evolved by the farmers in their field; or is a wild relative or land race of a variety about which the farmers possess the common knowledge.	Unclear if Distinctness, Uniformity and Stability would be the criteria or not.	Unclear	Unclear
Essentially Derived Variety	S2(i)	A variety predominantly derived from such initial variety, or from a variety that itself is predominantly derived from such initial variety, while retaining the expression of the essential characteristics that result from the genotypes of such initial variety; is clearly distinguishable from such initial variety;	Genera or species specified by the Central Government and tests to determine if it is an EDV.	Same rights as a breeder of a new variety provided that the authorization by the breeder of the initial variety to the breeder of essentially derived variety may be subject to terms mutually agreed upon by both the parties.	Initially 9 years renewable up to total of 18 years for trees and vines. Initially 6 years renewable up to total of 15 for other crops.

and conforms (except for the differences which result from the act of derivation) to such initial variety in the expression of the essential characteristics that result from the genotype or combination of genotypes of such initial variety.

Source : Adapted from "The Protection of Plant Varieties and Farmers' Rights Act, 2001" (Act No. 53 of 2001), New Delhi: Universal Law Publishing Co. Pvt. Ltd.

DIAGRAM 1
Likely Benefits to Actors from Various Types of Protection

Actor		*Variety*
Private Sector	⟶	New Variety
Public Sector	⟶	Extant Variety Essentially Derived Variety
NGO's/Farmers	⟶	Extant Variety Farmers' Variety Essentially Derived Variety.

1. New Variety

Protection of new varieties is the type of right demanded by breeders and generally refers to varieties protected under existing plant breeders' rights systems. The criteria for new varieties in India's Act are borrowed largely from UPOV and it would be mainly private sector breeders who could apply for protection of their innovations. Public sector institution and universities could also claim protection under this clause if they can innovate and produce new varieties.

2. Essentially Derived Variety

The concept of essentially derived variety first emerged when UPOV was revised in 1991. In India's legislation, the concept is modified to suit certain interests. The concept of EDV emerged in UPOV 1991 to ensure breeders greater protection by extending the scope of the initial breeder's right to varieties that are essentially derived from the protected variety. In India's legislation, the provision seems to have been adopted with the view that it could provide some protection to varieties held with the public sector. The Head of Seed Science Technology at the Indian Agriculture Research Institute pointed out that the provision was intended to 'provide protection for varieties developed by the public sector that have been acquired by the private sector and modified slightly'.[1] It is also interesting to note that some NGOs have

1. Seshia, 2001.

also been supportive of the EDV provision, in spite of the fact that it actually emerged to grant greater rights to breeders. M.S. Swaminathan at one point stated that "We should include in the 'essentially derived' concept the parent genetic material contributed by rural and tribal men and women", although the concept was not included in the draft produced by the Swaminathan Foundation.[2] This definition of EDV was also not included in India's Act. NGOs that have the capacity to modify varieties could perhaps utilize the provision and gain protection for them under the Act, and it could also be used to make claims for varieties that are used as initial varieties in breeding programs.

3. Extant Variety

Protection for extant varieties is a new criteria not found anywhere in the world. It is an attempt to extend protection to existing varieties rather than for newly developed innovations. Such protection facilitates the 'extraction of rents from old innovations'.[3] The provision for granting protection to *extant varieties* in India's plant variety legislation does not have a parallel in history and doesn't fit into the theoretical framework governing IPP.[4] The following are defined as extant varieties in India's Act : (1) varieties notified under the Seeds Act, (2) Farmers' Variety, variety in public domain, variety about which there is common knowledge. The extant variety need not show novelty and the criteria of distinctness, uniformity and stability (DUS) will be determined as specified under the regulations made by the Authority.[5] These specifications have not yet been formulated. The ability of farmers to actually register their varieties in practice depends on the definition of DUS that would be adopted. If the Authority adopts the same criteria applied to breeders' rights, then very few farmers would be able to register their varieties. It is clear that the public sector would be able to utilize the provision as it includes varieties notified under the Seeds Act.

2. Swaminathan, 1994.
3. Srinivasan, 2001 quoted in Seshia, 2001.
4. Economic and Social Commission for Asia and the Pacific, 2001.
5. Gopalkrishnan, 2001.

4. Farmers' Variety

The provision for protecting farmers' variety is most unique aspect of India's law. It is clear that this provision emerged to satisfy the interests of NGOs and farmers' lobbies who demanded that farmers should be treated on par with breeders and allowed to register their varieties. The provision for protecting farmers' variety represents the extension of private property constructs first developed for new varieties to varieties held by farmers and communities. It represents the expansion of farmers' rights from farmers' privilege and benefit sharing to granting ownership rights for farmers. Confusion however persists on the criteria that would be used for registering such varieties and it is not clear if the distinction, uniformity and stability criteria would be required or not. The Act states that "any farmer or group of farmers or community of farmers claiming to be a breeder of the variety"[6] can apply for registration of their varieties. Various NGOs can also have plans to register varieties on behalf of communities. The legislation also establishes various other provisions for protecting traditional varieties such as benefit sharing and a National Gene Fund. The new law sets-up a system of benefit sharing based on claims made by person/ NGOs in India to the Authority and determined by the Authority. Compensation can be claimed if person/community has contributed significantly to the evolution of a variety registered under the Act. The amount of benefit sharing would be deposited in the National Gene Fund and would be recoverable as an arrear of land revenue by the District Magistrate.

2. ANTICOMMONS ?

The new regime, in its attempts to equitably distribute rights, raises the possibility of an "anti-commons" situation taking shape. The tragedy of the anti-commons refers to the obstacles that arise when a user needs access to multiple protected inputs to create a single useful product.[7] A complex

6. S 16(1)(d) of the PVPFR Act, 2001.
7. Heller and Eisenberg, 1998.

series of bargaining with several actors may be required for development of new products under the new scenario. The following diagram illustrates the various levels of bargaining that may arise:

DIAGRAM 2
Stakeholder and Varietal Product under India's Law

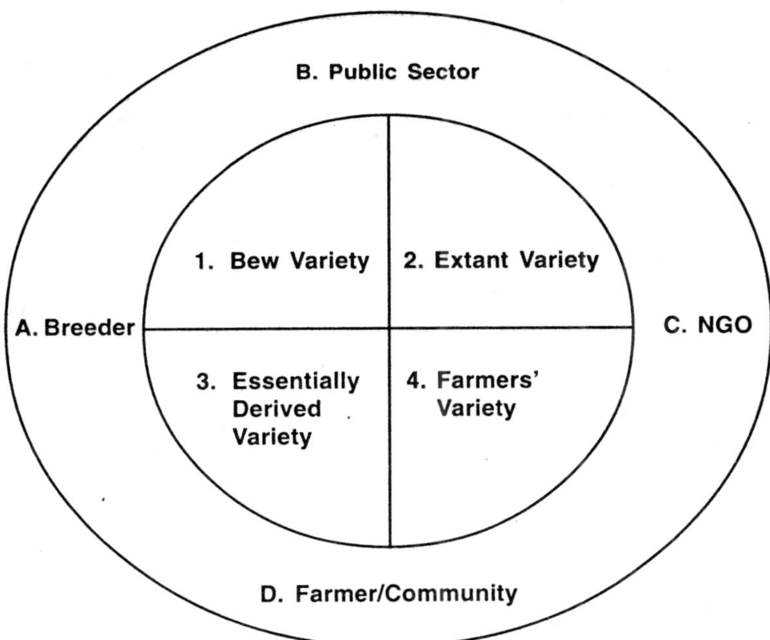

The quadrants represent the four types of varieties that can be registered and the various stakeholders. The actors in the outer circle can claim rights on varieties in any of the quadrants. An application for any type (New Variety, Farmers' Variety, Extant Variety, EDV) that requires use of a variety protected under another type would require payment and bargaining for commercialization. This creates a number of possibilities in terms of negotiations that may be required for creating the product. For example, let us take the breeder who applies for registration of a New Variety. If breeding this variety requires use of any of the other materials (varieties) in any of the other quadrants, he/she must bargain with that actor who has registered that variety and pay for use of that variety. Taking one actor (breeder) and one variety (new variety), based on one other registered variety, the following combinations may be possible:

Actors	*Varieties*
A, B	1, 2 (New variety based on extant variety registered by public sector).
B, C	1, 3 (New variety based on EDV registered by NGO).
A, D	1, 4 (New variety based on Farmers' Variety registered by community).

The breeder would have to bargain with the actor if he/she intended to commercialize the variety. If the bargaining fails, the result could be lack of investment and production of that commodity (i.e. anti-commons tragedy). Here the case of only one actor and one variety based on another variety is considered, but this becomes much more complex when one considers that actually there could be more than one variety used in creating the new variety or that many more actors may have gained ownership rights over the other varieties. Potentially, a specific agricultural resource could be protected under a number of mechanisms, and various actors could claim ownership over a particular aspect relating to the resource. An actor interested in utilizing a resource may have to gain permission from several actors and negotiate on a number of levels that may not be practically feasible. The result could be under utilization of the resource.

Overlapping claims are a distinct possibility within this system. It is possible to envisage a situation where various actors could gain protection in different forms on aspects of the same resource. Here, the example of ground nut variety is taken but almost any resource could be substituted.

A breeder could obtain a plant breeders' right for new variety of groundnut, for example, HYV ground nut. A public sector organization could claim protection for an extant variety of groundnut and an essentially derived variety of groundnut.

DIAGRAM 3

Forms of Protection Over Resources in India's Law

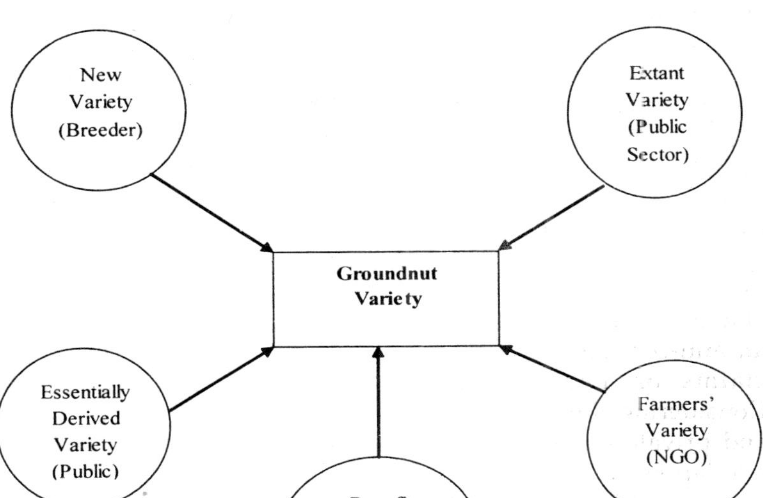

An NGO that is able to meet the criteria of DUS through some innovation of a groundnut variety could claim it as a farmers' variety. A community could also claim some aspect of benefit sharing because of use of the local variety in any of the other rights granted.

Here, only one actor within each category (private, public, etc.) is shown, but one could imagine a scenario where several private and public sector institutions could claim rights. Each actor would claim a different variety of groundnut so why should this create an anticommons situation? Although each actor claims rights over specific aspects of the resource it is clear that at least at some point of time, the actor would most probably have utilized the variety belonging to at least one of the other actors. In order to gain access to that variety a complex system of bargaining and payment would have to be initiated. In addition, any one actor who wants to utilize the resource would have to initiate bargaining with a number of actors. The transaction costs of such bargaining may lead to underutilization of the resource.

The enforcement of the law will also influence the scope of an anti-commons situation. An anti-commons situation perhaps may not arise if farmers/NGOs are unable to assert rights over farmers' varieties. Yet there is scope for an anti-commons situation not only because of the extension of rights of farmers, but also due to the nature of varieties that can be protected under this law. India's law differs from western IPR systems in allowing for various forms of protection such as extant varieties. Even if only the public and private sectors are able to actually enforce their rights leaving out farmers/NGOs, an anti-commons situation could take place with overlapping claims on new varieties, extant varieties, and EDVs. Considering the existing patterns of exchange between public and private sectors in India, there is enormous scope for such overlapping claims. NGOs are already preparing for the new regime and have documented a number of resource that could be registered under the law. The inability of small farmers to enforce their rights may lead to a situation where public sector, private sector and NGOs are engaged in a tussle to claims rights. In the middle of this struggle, farmers may themselves be denied access to their own varieties. The result could be underutilization of the resource both due to anti-commons tragedy (if NGOs, public sector and breeders are claiming various rights over the same resources) and lack of access to the resource for farmers.

3. IMPACT ON FLOW OF RESOURCES

The impact of the new legislation on the flow of resources between actors is not easy to determine, but it is clear that it would significantly alter existing patterns of exchange. One school of thought points to the increase in access to the best and recently bred foreign varieties with the extension of PBRs in developing countries.[8] The logic is that MNCs would

8. Arora quoted in Weidlich, 1996.

introduce new varieties in India with the protection afforded by IPRs against copying of their material. The introduction of new varieties by private firms is dependent on several factors apart from intellectual property protection and would therefore require deeper study. However, it is clear that the new IPR regime would alter the existing patterns of exchange dramatically. It is important to analyze these changes and their implications :

Public Sector ——————→ CGIAR

Indian public sector institutions currently transfer material freely to the CGIAR and also receive such material from the International Agriculture Research Centres. Under the new regime, however, India's public sector institutions would have the ability to charge for the use of material that could be registered under the Act. Since CGIAR centers currently operate on the basis of free exchange, there may arise greater incentives to transfer material to actors who would pay for the resource rather than to the international agricultural centers. This would also depend on some extent on the implementation of FAO's recently concluded International Treaty on Plant Genetic Resources. India could also charge for exchanges between countries that do not go through the CG system. Foreign actors would also be able to register their varieties in India and charge for use.

Public Sector ——————→ Private Sector

Under India's system, the public sector has freely transferred material to the private sector. With the capacity to protect both new varieties and extant varieties under the Act, there could be certain changes to this practice of free exchange. The access of small seed companies to this material may be reduced if these firms would not be able to afford payment for the use of this material. Large seed companies may not be hindered from access for monetary reasons but would have to negotiate the terms for such access. If the bargaining fails or is not easily facilitated, the exchange of resources may be restricted.

Public Sector ——————→ Farmers

The public sector institutions in India transfer many seeds and varieties to farmers and this constitutes an important system of free exchange. Under the new regime, if the public sector finds it can earn revenue from the private sector for use of its varieties, it may rather charge for use of its varieties from the private sector rather than giving it away freely to farmers.

Farmer ——————→ Farmer

The importance of farmer-to-farmer exchange of seeds has been stated as one of the reasons for upholding farmers' rights under any breeders' legislation in India. According to Suman Sahai of the Gene Campaign, "Over 85% of the seeds amounting to roughly 52 lakh tons, that are planted in Indian fields every year are supplied by the farming community".[9] The new legislation ensures that farmers have the right to exchange seeds and would not be prevented from sharing seeds with other farmers provided he/she does not sell the seed as a brand name (the breeders' registered name). However, the incentive to share seed would also be influenced by the ability to claim ownership rights over farmers' variety provided under the Act. If it becomes possible for farmers to register their varieties under the Act, they would have a greater incentive to charge for use of the variety rather than giving it away freely to other farmers.

The direct exchange between farmers to farmers may also be mediated by a relatively new actor-NGOs-in the system. It is not yet clear what would be the impact of NGOs on exchange of plant genetic resources between the stakeholders, but it is important to note that they would play a significant role in the new regime.

1. Preliminary Evidence

At this point it is difficult to find conclusive evidence of the impact of this legislation as it is in the process of being implemented. However, it is possible to see from several

9. Sahai, 2000.

TABLE 6.2
Documentation of Genetic Resources/Traditional Knowledge

Activity and Year Launched	*Agency*	*Description*
(1)	*(2)*	*(3)*
National Biodiversity and Strategy Action Plan, 1999	Ministry of Environment and Forests, UNDP, Kalpraviksh and Biotech Consortium India Limited	Assessment and stocktaking of biodiversity-related information at national, local and state levels
National Innovation Foundation, 2000	Department of Science and Technology and IIM, Ahmedabad	Register and support grassroots innovations
Biodiversity Plan	Government of Karnataka	State laws regarding biodiversity
Biodiversity Plan	Government of Kerala	State laws regarding biodiversity
Mission Mode Project on Collection, Documentation and validation of indigenous technical knowledge	Indian Council of Agricultural Research	Documentation and registration of traditional knowledge
Traditional Knowledge Digital Library	Council of Scientific and Industrial Research	International Library on traditional knowledge
People's Biodiversity Registers, 1995	Foundation for Revitalisation of Local Health Traditions	Records the status, uses and management of living resources

(*Contd.*)

TABLE 6.2 (Contd.)

(1)	(2)	(3)
Honeybee Network, 1996	Sristi	Document innovative practices of farmers/artisans
Database	Swaminathan Foundation	Document contributions of tribal groups for securing benefits
Documentation	Research Foundation, Green Foundation, Gene Campaign	Documenting and collecting traditional knowledge/resources
Village Registry, 1997	Pattuvam Village, Kerala	Produced a registry of genetic resources within their village and declared it their property

Source : Compiled from various sources including www.sristi.org, Gadgil et al, New Meaning for old knowledge: The People's Biodiversity Registers Programme, paper for Ecological Applications; Government of India, 2000, National Biodiversity Strategy and Action Plan: Guidelines and Concept Papers; Government of Karnataka, Biodiversity Plan.

developments, the future implications for stakeholder access. Firstly, several actors have already begun the process of asserting rights over resources that were in the public domain. The process of documenting genetic resources in India has taken an enormous momentum. Registers to document such resources are being taken up by various actors including governments at the National, State and Local level, Public sector institutions and non-governmental organizations. These registers are being developed in an *ad hoc* manner, and there is a great deal of duplication of efforts and overlap not only in terms of resources but also regions covered. It is clear that those documenting resources would seek to apply for registration under the new Act where ever possible under the four types of varieties protectable under the Act. The number of documenting activities and their scope reveal the complexities that may arise when actors would attempt to acquire rights under the Act. The following table outlines the number of documentation activities in India.

These documentation activities would obviously be aimed at securing some protection either through plant variety or farmers rights protection. In addition, the resources being documented here extend beyond plant genetic material and also include indigenous practices and traditional knowledge. It is unclear how such claims would be treated as traditional knowledge is not defined in this law explicitly and the law is mainly focused on varietal protection. There are serious demands in India for establishing another law to deal exclusively with traditional knowledge, with some efforts being made to draft a legislation in this regard.

The extent of these documentation activities indicates that a number of actors documenting a variety of resources could file claims both for benefit sharing and for registering of varieties under the Act. These could be done under the following provisions of the Act: (1) Extant Variety if it meets the criteria of DUS as specified by the Authority (2) Farmers' Variety depending on the criteria that it would be based on. It may also be possible to file an application under the other two types if some actors are able to innovate on existing varieties to produce a New Variety or an EDV. There could also be

TABLE 6.3
Resources Under Documentation

Program	*Resources being Documented*	*Area*
(1)	*(2)*	*(3)*
National Biodiversity and Strategy Action Plan	Distribution of economic and endangered species, site-specific threats and pressures, social/political/economic issues, ethical concerns and ongoing conservation initiatives by various sections of society.	20 local-level action plans, 30 state-level plans, 10 inter-state eco-regional plans 13 national thematic plans, all of these building into an overview national plan, but also remaining independent action plans.
National Innovation Foundation (NIF)	Grassroots innovations	Not specified
People's Biodiversity Register	Documents folk ecological knowledge and wisdom through decentralized institutions of governance, and with the help of local level educational institutions.	First initiatives: 24 sites covering 10 states, second phase: 10 sites in 4 states, third phase: 56 sites in 7 states. 75 plant biodiversity registers covering 10 states of India produced by mid-1998.
Sristi	Surveyed about 4500 villages and documented more than 10,000 innovations related to agriculture, livestock health and management, farm implements and machinery, poultry keeping, leather tanning, herbal medicine, vegetable dye, etc.	As of 1996, 5376 innovative practices (from about 3500 farmers and artisans of about 2300 villages) had been documented. Currently there are about 8,000 innovations and about 10,000 practices that have been recorded. Database on medicinal plants of about 256 plants found and locally used by farmers.

Source : Compiled from various sources including www.sristi.org, Gadgil *et. al.*, New Meanings for old knowledge: The People's Biodiversity Registers Programme, paper for Ecological Applications; Government of India, 2000, National Biodiversity Strategy and Action Plan: Guidelines and Concept Papers; Government of Karnataka, Biodiversity Plan.

many claims for benefit sharing if any of these materials are used in the production of any type of variety.

Recent patent applications in India relating to some agricultural commodities compared with the documentation activities taking place point to the type of overlapping claims that could arise. Since applications for registering varieties under the Act are yet to be made, patent applications are used as an indication of the type of agricultural resources that may be the source of new innovations leading to creation of new varieties that can be protected under the Act. The following table lists the number of patent applications filed in India on some selected commodities:

TABLE 6.4

Patent Applications Related to Specific Agricultural Products, January 1995-June 2000

Commodity	*Number of Applications*
Rice	60
Cotton	51
Neem	47
Wheat	6
Sunflower	2
Tomato	4
Maize	4
Cauliflower	1
Sugarcane	14
Corn	5

Source : Calculated from TIFAC (1998 updated 2001). Database on Patent Applications Filed in India.

To analyze the means by which various actors could attempt to file applications relating to the same resources we focus on potential overlapping between patent applications and documentation activities. A search in just one of the documentation databases, the National Innovation Foundation shows that registration relating to neem, rice and cotton exists

in this database. The Sristi database illustrates even more sharply the nature of duplication that could occur. The following table illustrates the large number of references found to three products: neem, rice and cotton in the Sristi database:

TABLE 6.5
Sristi Database

Commodity	*No. of Entries*
Neem	95
Rice	105
Cotton	94

Source : www.sristi.org

The number of references to these resources illustrates that duplication of ownership claims that could occur not only between different types of protection systems (patents, plant breeders' rights, farmers' variety, extant varieties and EDVs) but also between various actors filing for claims relating to the same product. This would create not only serious administrative difficulties, but could also lead to situations where bargaining and negotiations would be required to commercialize a product from many actors who each make claims to specific aspects of the resource. In the extreme case, an anti-commons tragedy could result where resources remain underutilized due to the existence of multiple ownership rights.

4. POLICY IMPLICATIONS

The danger of a situation arising where resources remain underutilized cannot be ignored. One may argue that market mechanisms would evolve to ensure that an 'anti-commons' situation does not arise in India. However, several obstacles seem to prevent the emergence of market mechanisms to facilitate collaboration in this case (for obstacles in the case of agricultural biotechnology.[10] This section draws from their

10. See Heller and Eisenberg, 1998.

observations, applying similar analogies). High transaction costs of bargaining appear to be a major impediment to overcoming the anticommons tragedy in India. Firstly, many of the owners in the new IPR regime will be actors that have limited resources for absorbing transaction costs and limited competence in market-oriented bargaining. These include public sector institutions, local communities, non-governmental organizations and farmers. Secondly, since the rights cover such a vast arena of resources and practices, comparing values would make it difficult to evolve a standard distribution scheme. Thirdly, costly case-by-case negotiations may be required since there are no standard license terms for such collaborations. Fourthly, licensing transaction costs are likely to arise in the early stage as the outcome or gains from use of the resource are speculative.

One of the major factors that may present the anti-commons tragedy in this case is the interests of actors. Firstly, there are a variety of actors with different goals involved. The goals of the public and private sector may vary, and certainly interests of non-governmental organizations and firms may prevent collaboration. Secondly, the terms of negotiations of these actors would not be on the same level. A farmer may seek a totally different outcome than a breeder or firm. Thirdly, an actor may perceive the collaboration to be against his/her interests. For example, the public sector may not be interested in giving materials to a company that would be its competitor on a particular technology. Some communities may be interested in keeping their knowledge secret, especially if the incentive (monetary) may not be of much value to them. Under the new regime, actors may overvalue their assets preventing smooth bargaining. When it is not clear what the value of genetic resource is, and under a competitive environment, actors may place too much value on their assets. If each owner overestimates the value of his/her resources, the actors may not be able to reach consensus on a sharing agreement leading to the product not being developed.

Bureaucratic procedure for obtaining access may prohibit sharing of resources. This is a serious problem under India's new regime. The new Act establishes an Authority to administer the legislation. The emergence of a new bureaucratic organization to regulate ownership rights in areas that were in the public domain creates possibilities for delays and hindrances in the free flow of resources between actors. It must also be viewed in the context of the new IPR regime being established in India with greater role for the Patent Office and the plans for setting up another authority under the Biological Diversity Act, recently passed in India. The emergence of new authorities to regulate ownership rights, benefit sharing and access to genetic resources presents the danger of an anticommons tragedy. Two new central boards are planed: (1) Protection of Plant Varieties and farmers' Rights Authority, (2) National Biodiversity Authority. In addition, several State Biodiversity Boards would also be established and the powers of the Patent Office would be expanded. Securing rights and negotiating licenses may involve numerous agencies and actors. This could be an impediment to sharing and effective utilization of resources.

These factors point to a clear need for public policy interventions to promote the utilization and flow of resources. There are some policies that could be pursued towards this goal. Firstly, devising clear-cut MTA (Material Transfer Agreement) is essential. MTAs determine the basis on which negotiations can take place between actors. Public sector organizations, NGOs and private sector firms need to set down guidelines for negotiations on transfer of materials. Secondly, it would be necessary to devote some attention to ensuring that there are adequate resources in the public domain. India has recently ratified FAO's International Treaty on Plant Genetic Resources which attempts to set-up a multilateral system of exchange of crops. It would be important for India to closely study the implications in this treaty and establish mechanisms for ensuring that certain crops remain in the public domain.[11] Thirdly, it would be necessary to limit the extent of protection available under the Act. This could be done through exemptions in the Act based on public interest or more specifically by establishing more stringent criteria for gaining protection. Finally, there must be some attention to creating incentives for sharing resources other than

11. Ramanna, 2001.

monetary gain through proprietary rights. India's public sector agricultural research has witnessed a number of successes largely due to the ability to freely exchange resources. The important flow of resources between the public sector and farmers and farmers themselves must continue. In order for this to occur, actors must be provided incentives to share rather than only gains from asserting exclusionary rights through the Act.

India's Plant Variety and Farmers' Rights Act is significant both in the domestic and international context. The possibility of a domestic anti-commons situation arising takes on even greater proportions at the international level. Several developing countries are currently formulating legislations to simultaneously conform to TRIPs, while regulating access to genetic resources and granting some form of farmers' rights. Developing nations are not implementing straight-jacket fitting rules found in TRIPs, but are creating structures that reflect provisions found in the Convention on Biological Diversity, the international movement on farmers' rights, and applying property right constructs to resources found in their territories. Advanced nations must recognize that compelling developing countries to grant breeders' rights could result in systems that run counter to their interests. Developing nations, in seeking to achieve the important goal of recognizing farmers' rights, must not overlook the need for promoting exchange of agricultural resources. Developed and developing countries must make a concerted effort to ensure that emerging IPR regimes do not restrict stakeholder access to genetic resources.

7

Conclusion and Suggestions

1. CONCLUSION

The foregoing 'discussion and analysis made in this book reveals that the economic reforms announced by the government have changed the direction of the country from the socialistic pattern to the market driven economy. Under the influence of globalization a transition is gradually taking place in the role of the state from active regulator to passive intervener in the spheres of social, economic, agrarian and industrial relations. A clear shift in the governmental attitude from being a close ally of the farmers for the last forty years and more, to becoming a strong promoter of the industry, leaving the underdog to fend for itself can easily be seen. This transformation creates new complexities and challenges in the agrarian relations leading to a discernable crisis in agrarian relations.

Since the Government is now recasting its role in tune with on-going economic transformation and new economic regime, it cannot be expected to continue its active role in future.

However, as India is in the midst of implementing Structural Adjustment reforms, a sudden withdrawal of the policies cannot be expected and it is too late to go for a reversal of the globalization process. So pragmatism demands initiating necessary measures to counter the negative impacts of these economic policy reforms. It would be apt here to quote the former Prime Minister P.V. Narasimha Rao, from his address to the World economic forum at Davos, Switzerland, in February 1994, that "Change has to be accepted as a result of deliberate and objective thinking. In the new-found enthusiasm for change, governments should not go overboard and plunge large chunks of their people into mass misery; they have no right to do that . . . each society has to find its own 'middle way' suited to its genius and circumstances; and, this should be the approach that accepts change".[1] Clearly the Indian case—in terms of both magnitude and complexity of the challenges—calls for a different strategy than elsewhere. This change in the attitude is clearly not in consonance with the ideals of socio-economic justice inherent in the Constitution of India. As observed by the Supreme Court of India:

> "Freedom of trade does not mean freedom to exploit. The provisions of the Constitution are not erected as barriers to progress. They provide a plan for orderly progress towards the social order contemplated by the preamble to the Constitution. They do not permit any kind of slavery, social, economic or political."[2]

According to the Noble Laureate economist Prof. Amartya Sen, the State has greater responsibility and not a minimal role in a democratic Government, which is honest and sensitive to the needs of the citizens. While supporting post-1991 economic liberalization polices, Professor Sen identifies "the central issue" as "expanding the social opportunities open to the

1. As quoted in C.S. Venkataratnam: 'Giobalisition and Labour-Management Relation : Dynamics of Change', 2001, p. 22.
2. Chandra Bhavan Boarding and Lodging *v.* The State of Maysore, 1970, 2. S.C.R. 600.

people." He stressed the need for social safety nets to profit from globalisation.[3]

For welfare States, social justice must be an integral part of all developmental planning. Approaches such as, growth first and justice later are as contentious as, 'chicken or egg, which came first?" Exhortations by political leaders to 'sacrifice today for a better tomorrow' fall on deaf ears in societies where the rich continue to get richer and the poor poorer. As the United Nations Development Programme, 1987 (UNDP) declared, "Economic development should be the means and social development should be the goal."[4]

Very recently, the then Prime Minister of India, Shri A.B.Vajpayee, while addressing the Asian Summit on Youth Entrepreneurship and Employment on October 30, 2003 at New Delhi, opined that "Both globally and locally, we have to reorient our economic thinking, planning and implementation to achieve the goal of full employment everywhere. We should be prepared to reform anything that needs to be reformed to achieve this central goal—be it the global financial architecture, the world trade regime, or the growth-obstructing laws and institutions at national and local levels".[5]

It is, therefore, submitted that while making any attempt to reform anything the Government and policy makers should keep in mind the postulates of economic and social policies envisaged by the Constitution. Otherwise, the reformatory process will lead to a serious constitutional crisis and further hamper social harmony and the progress of the nation.

Finally, the following inferences can be drawn from the discussions and analysis made in this work.

The economic reforms announced by the Government under the influence of globalization process has changed the policy directions of the country from socialistic pattern to market economy. The dominant role played by the state, since independence, in social, economic, agrarian and industrial

3. See Jean Dre'ze and Amartya Sen: 'India Economic Development and Social Opportunity', 1995 and See also *The Hindu*, dt. 10th June, 1999 and January 5, 2004.
4. *Supra* Note 1 at p. 166.
5. *Yojana*, December, 2003, p. 26.

relations fields seems to be diminishing. The country is forced to opt for a residual model where the State accepts no direct responsibility for ensuring the well-being of its people. As a result, the entire policy directions of the State becomes incompatible with the policy prescriptions of the Indian Constitution.

The introduction of diverse forms of intellectual property rights in the agricultural field is on the whole completely novel in India and mainly linked to the necessity to comply with India's existing international obligations and to the general trend towards the privatization of knowledge in recent decades. This new system is in complete contradiction with the previous system of agricultural management which privileged the sharing of resources and knowledge concerning plant varieties by all actors from local farmers to those at the international level. In this context, while individual property rights over state-of-the-art inventions are being strengthened in large part in response to WTO related obligations, the development of strong and effective farmers' rights is of increasing importance. This should allow them to defend their interests against fraudulent appropriation and to allow them to defend their own knowledge in a legal ands commercial sense if they so wish. Farmers' rights should, however, not be conceived strictly along the lines of existing intellectual property rights such as patents and plant breeders' rights. In fact, while the commercialization of food crops may be important to all actors engaged in agriculture management, it is by far not the only relevant consideration. Much broader issues such as the conservation and sustainable use of agro-biodiversity and food security for each and every individual are as important and probably much more central than commercial considerations in a field which directly concerns the fulfilment of basic food needs. In this sense, the introduction of farmers' rights fulfils a number of significant functions from a socio-ecological point of view:

- Farmers' rights contribute to making the legal system fairer by providing property rights to all relevant actors in plant variety management.

- Farmers' rights contribute to the recognition of the contribution of farmers to food security, to conservation and sustainable agro-biodiversity management and to innovation in agricultural management; and finally,
- Farmers' rights will make an enormous contribution to food security by fostering control, not only over resources and land but also over knowledge for the dozens of crops of people who are directly engaged in small-scale agricultural management.

Conversely, the development of farmers' rights provides an opportunity to re-examine patents and plant breeders' rights. This should contribute to make these more 'traditional' intellectual property rights more relevant to the field of agriculture by, for instance, imposing new conditions on rights holders concerning both traditional knowledge and biodiversity conservation.

As a result of international obligations in this field and with a view to foster food security, a comprehensive plant variety protection regime should include the following elements:

- The protection of commercially relevant knowledge;
- The conservation and management of biological resources and genetic resources;
- The protection through property rights of traditional knowledge; and
- The recognition that plant variety management and protection should be intrinsically linked to the fundamental human right to food.

In other words, a legal regime concerning plant varieties should not stop at what is commercially useful today but should incorporate, for instance, human rights consideration

2. SUGGESTIONS

Some indication of the possible shape of a comprehensive farmers' rights regime at the domestic level can be given:

1. Farmers' rights should be conceived as a positive mechanism giving traditional knowledge-holders' property rights and therefore full control over their knowledge. This involves allowing farmers to commercialise their own knowledge. In this sense, farmers' rights are based on the recognition that all economic actors should have commercial rights over their knowledge, and not only one specific category of inventors. A further justification for the introduction of farmers' rights is the role that property rights play in fostering the sustainable use and the conservation of resources due to the intrinsic link between the knowledge and the resource and the requirement of ownership of both to foster their conservation. In this sense, farmers' rights are perfectly suited to play a multiple role in granting full property rights to farmers which allow commercialization if desired, in contributing to agro-biodiversity conservation, and simultaneously fostering food security at the local level. Overall, farmers' rights should be conceived from the point of view of farmers and in accordance with their view of sustainability and commercial use. If this is not achieved, there is a significant danger that farmers' rights will be used only as a way to force poor farmers to maintain agro-biodiversity for the global good of humankind with minimal personal rewards.
2. In the context of the multiple goals of farmers' rights, other actors involved in agro-biodiversity management should also have duties towards the promotion of food security, agro-biodiversity conservation and sustainable use. While farmers directly benefit from agro-biodiversity conservation, the global community also benefits in direct and indirect ways. This calls for the sharing of conservation obligations on an equitable basis between all actors benefiting from the exploitation of agro-biodiversity. This burden should not only be spread amongst farmers and local firms marketing seeds, foodstuffs and other crops but also at the

international level, given that outside firms, individuals and eventually the international community benefit from these conservation activities.

3. The question of the introduction of farmers' rights includes important issues concerning the holders of the rights. Intellectual property rights such as patents are often conceived as purely individual rights even though in practice, they can easily be shared among several individuals or entities. Intellectual property rights can less easily lend themselves to shared management in the case of an unidentifiable number of rights holders. Farmers' rights present specific problems in this field. In some instances, specific individuals may make individual contributions to the development of a new or improved plant variety. In this situation, the model provided by individual rights can be applied in the case of farmers' rights. This case is, however, likely to be most infrequent given that novelty is very often the product of direct or indirect collaboration between different individuals and/or communities. As a result, farmers' rights are likely to be of communal nature. The usual intellectual property rights model is not well suited to the recognition of common property rights over knowledge because it generally seeks to individualize contributions to the development of science and technology. As a result, it will be necessary to develop new tools to take into account the special nature of knowledge pertaining to plant genetic resources. Even in cases where contributions by specific individuals can be identified, it may not be equitable to assign rights to specific individuals because the subject matter of farmers' rights is closely linked to food security which is of direct interest to each and every individual in the local community and beyond. One way to solve the problem of allocation in countries like India which have institutions of local democratic governance is to determine that panchayats or their equivalent elsewhere should be the center/entity for locating

the ownership of farmers' rights. With appropriate safeguards to ensure that panchayats do not replicate economic inequalities between members of a local community, they can constitute an appropriate institutional framework for ensuring that everyone benefits from any existing entitlements. The rationale for not following the usual individual allocation model is that knowledge pertaining to plant genetic resources is directly related to the fulfilment of basic food needs for all individuals, landowners, farmers, manual labour and non-farming individuals in a given community. Farmers' rights seek to give control to individual and local communities over their knowledge and resources. This does not imply that the rights conferred must be to the exclusion of any other similar right elsewhere. In terms of the possible commercialization of the product, this indicates that instead of a monopoly right, all rights holders are entitled to separately manufacture and commercialise their own products without infringing anyone's right.

4. The question arises of the uses to which farmers' rights can be put. From a broad perspective, these can be summarized under 'defensive' and 'positive' functions. The former will be there to help farmers fight the appropriation of their resources and knowledge with legal tools. Today, the whole of "traditional knowledge" is deemed to be in the public domain because it cannot be assigned towards re-establishing a fair playing field in which all actors have claims over their knowledge, farmers' rights will also constitute the basis for claims of benefit-sharing as recognized at the national levels. The positive function of farmers' rights is the most innovative and important in the long-run. In a world where all resources and knowledge are being assigned, it is imperative for reasons of equity and food security that farmers and farming communities acquire control sanctioned by the law as this constitutes one of the few ways in which incentives

for agro-biodiversity conservation and innovation at the local level can be maintained. The commercial use of the protective knowledge may serve as an added bonus which traditional knowledge-holders may or may not use.

Farmers' Rights as of now does not entail, in legal terms, a "right" and a related "obligation" (because the International undertaking adopted by the FAO conference in 1983 is a non-binding instrument),[6] but only the acceptance of the notion that such a right should be recognized and implemented. If Farmers' Rights were to become effective legal rights, there must exist an obligation imposed on all or some third parties. There is no right without a corresponding enforceable obligation. Very different views have been expressed with respect to the content of the rights to be conferred, and on whom these rights should be conferred (national governments, the international community, or both), and by whom they should be realized. According to Riley[7] for instance, the realization of Farmers' Rights should mean the recognition of the rights to:

- save seeds;
- have access to "the latest technology";[8]
- receive information on and duplicate samples of the materials collected by third parties;
- receive public credit for having provided genetic resources; and
- contribute to or facilitating the realization of public sector plant breeding and agricultural research objectives.

---

6. The current negotiations for the revision of the International Undertaking may conclude, however, with the adoption of a binding instrument, possibly a Protocol to the CBD.
7. Riley, 1996, p. 59.
8. It may be noted, however, that it may be extremely difficult to satisfy this demand, and that traditional farmers generally do not need the latest technology.

The following proposals may be made for ensuring effective Farmers' rights including different kinds of rights/ obligations that may constitute the basis of those Rights. Such proposals include the following possible measures.

1. By the International Community

Assistance to Governments

- Assistance by the international community, as a beneficiary of the PGR developed and conserved by farmers, should be given to national governments for the purpose of ensuring/encouraging equitable benefits to present and future generations of farmers and farming (and indigenous) communities.

Support of Farmers

- By establishing an international fund and developing its operational mechanism: to ensure conservation and sustainable use of plant genetic resources, and traditional farmers' knowledge; to facilitate and ensure access to new technologies and equitable sharing of benefits derived from the products obtained through the use of plant genetic resources for the benefit of present and future generations of farmers; and to make appropriate efforts to mobilize adequate financial resources to support farmers' activities to conserve and use sustainably plant genetic resources for food and agriculture; and
- By ensuring that international aid programmes benefit farmers by furthering their activities to conserve and sustainably use plant genetic resources for food and agriculture.

Recognition of Rights in Knowledge

- By promoting the establishment of the development of an international *sui generis* system for the recognition, protection and compensation of knowledge, innovations and practices of farmers and traditional communities.

2. By National Governments

Assistance to Farmers and Promotional Measures

- Adoption of appropriate measures reflecting national capacities and needs, which are non-discriminatory and non-trade-distorting, and which are necessary for Parties and/or farmers to continue to conserve, manage and improve plant genetic resources for food and agriculture.
- Assistance to farmers and (traditional) farming communities, especially in areas of origin/diversity of plant genetic resources, in contributing to the evolution, conservation, improvement, evaluation and sustainable use of plant genetic resources for food and agriculture, through the participation in and establishment or strengthening of appropriate arrangements, and the participation of farmers and (traditional) farming communities therein such as:

  (i) national (and regional) germplasm programmes; and
  (ii) initiatives that promote the use of, and research into, crops which are not widely used.

- Adoption of support measures for research, training and institutional capacity building activities at the local level, with the participation of the communities concerned, particularly focusing on women farmers, and measures for credit facilities and market provisions governing farmers' access to plant genetic resources for enhancing traditional genetic resources, development and the exchange systems through, *inter alia,* the removal of financial and market barriers against such systems, for conservation, development and sustainable use, and transfer of technology that protect, integrate, enhance and develop traditional farmers' knowledge, know-how and practices.

- Ensuring that international aid programmes benefit farmers by furthering their activities to conserve and sustainably use plant genetic resources for food and agriculture.

Recognition of Rights in Knowledge

- To promote legal protection systems (and/or other mechanisms) on the national level in order to render effective the rights of farmers and the fair and equitable sharing of the benefits arising out of the utilization of plant genetic resources for food and agriculture.
- To establish national systems, including *sui generis* systems, as appropriate, to ensure/promote the fair and equitable sharing of the benefits arising out of the utilization of plant genetic resources for food and agriculture.
- To ensure that the (individual and/or) collective knowledge and plant genetic resources for food and agriculture held and developed by farmers and local farming communities are protected and promoted by adopting and implementing appropriate legislation in the form of collective rights regimes that provide for the adequate protection of traditional or indigenous knowledge, innovations, materials and practices of and by farmers and farming/local communities and promote the equitable sharing of benefits arising from the utilization of their plant genetic resources for food and agriculture.
- To review, assess and, if appropriate, modify intellectual property rights systems, land tenure, and seed laws in order to ensure their harmony with Farmers' Rights.

Prior Consent

- To ensure that the prior informed consent of the

concerned farmers and local communities is obtained before the collection of plant resources is undertaken; adapt current variety registration systems so as to identify and record, as appropriate, varieties of plant genetic resources provided by farmers and farming communities; and require disclosure of the origin of plant genetic resources utilized in the development of commercial varieties.

3. By National/International Action

- To enhance the productivity/efficiency of farmers by promoting the integration of farmers' traditional knowledge, know-how and practices, with modern technologies, as appropriate.
- To promote national and international scientific and technological agricultural research that supports and enhances, as appropriate, farmer-based knowledge systems related to plant genetic resources for food and agriculture.
- To recognize and protect the traditional rights of farmers and their communities to use, exchange, share and market their seeds/landraces and other plant reproductive material including the right to reuse farm-saved seed.
- To encourage/recognize and ensure the rights of farmers in sharing the benefits arising from the direct use of plant genetic resources on a fair and equitable basis including, through the transfer of technology, participation in research, and access to the results of research and development, where appropriate, derived at present and in the future, from the improved use of plant genetic resources through plant breeding and other modern scientific methods, as well as from their commercial use.
- To promote/ensure the participation of the farmers and local farming communities in the reviewing and implementation of measures provided under the International Undertaking and the International Fund which may/shall include the initiation of

flexible consultative processes to meet this aim and participation in the development and implementation of legislative measures on Farmers' Rights at national and international levels.

In sum, the proposals made during the revision of the International Undertaking indicate that Farmers' Rights may be realized through a variety of actions and measures at the national level. Possible options in this regard are further explored in the next Section.

3. A CONSENSUS TEXT : IMPLEMENTING FARMERS' RIGHTS AT THE NATIONAL LEVEL

The "Contact Group" established by the Chairman of the FAO Commission on Genetic Resources For Food and Agriculture in order to advance negotiations on the revision of the International Undertaking, agreed, during the Eighth Regular Session of the Commission (3-7 April 1999, Rome) on a text for Article 15 on "Farmers' Rights". This text (see Annexure I) stipulates that the responsibility for realizing Farmers' Rights rests with national governments, which should adopt, according to their needs and priorities, and subject to national laws, measures to protect traditional knowledge, benefit-sharing and to ensure the participation of farmers in decisions on PGRFA. The agreed text also clarifies that nothing in Article 15 will be interpreted as restricting the rights of the farmers to conserve, use, exchange and sell propagating material held on their farms, in accordance with national legislation.

The proposed text has found broad support among FAO member countries, including developed and developing countries alike.[9] Several elements of the agreed text need to be

9. See, for example, the Report of the Third Meeting of Commission I of the 30th Period of FAO Conference (Rome, 16 November 1999) and in particular the statements supporting the agreed text on Article 15 made by Turkey, Rep. of Korea, India and Finland (in the name of the European Community and its Member States), Algeria, Ethiopia, Norway, Republic of Congo and the United States, among others.

highlighted. In doing so, it is useful to compare the agreed draft text with the concepts contained in the Annexes to the Undertaking adopted through FAO Resolutions 4/89 and 5/89 (see Annexure II) which introduced the notion of Farmers' Rights.

First, the text recognizes the "enormous contribution" that has been made for the "conservation and development" of PGRFA, thus closely following point 3 of FAO Resolution 4/89. Second, while only "farmers" were mentioned in the Annexes to the International Undertaking, the agreed text alludes to "the local and indigenous communities and farmers", in line with the terminology of the CBD. This is a clear indicator of the growing recognition of the role played by such communities in the creation and preservation of knowledge of value for the society as a whole. Third, the agreed text states that the responsibility for realizing Farmers' Rights rests with national governments. This is a major difference compared with the original FAO text, which had emphasized the *global* nature of farmers' contributions and the primary role of the international community in realizing Farmers' Rights. FAO Resolutions 4/89 and 3/91 had established, in this regard, that Farmers' Rights would be implemented through an International Fund. However, the implementation has not yet materialized for the negotiators have apparently agreed not to insist on this idea.

It is clear in the agreed text that Farmers' Rights are to be established in accordance with "the needs and priorities" of each Party "as appropriate, and subject to its national legislation". Governments *should* (and not "shall") take certain measures. This means that the implementation of the measures indicated in paragraphs (a) to (c) will be largely dependent upon each governments' judgment on what is appropriate in the light of its own priorities and consistent with its national law. The nature and scope of the said Rights is, therefore, likely to differ significantly among countries. Some countries may, given the flexibility offered by the agreed text, even opt not to implement this provision.

The measures to be established must aim to "protect and promote" Farmers' Rights, that is, there should be measures relating to the legal recognition of such Rights as well as to encourage that they achieve their intended goals. It is important to note that paragraphs (a) to (c) of draft Article 15.2 are only *illustrative* of the measures that should be adopted, but they do not exhaust the list of modalities under which Farmers' Rights may be realized. The possible scope of such measures is examined below.

Finally, draft Article 15.3, offered by the United States delegation as a compromise solution, apparently satisfied those who expected a positive recognition under the revised International Undertaking of certain rights of farmers in relation to saving, using and exchanging seeds, and those who feared that the Undertaking could limit the breeders' rights that would be inconsistent with UPOV and UPOV-like legislation. The agreed draft text only states that Article 15 is *neutral* in that respect, that is, while it could not be a sufficient legal basis for claiming rights in relation to saving, using and exchanging seeds, at the same time Article 15 does not restrict the options that may be adopted by national governments in that regard. Clearly, the agreed text does not exclude the possibility that national laws (including PBRs and seed legislation) limit farmers' rights in relation to saving, using and exchanging seeds/propagating materials.

In the following sub-sections the different elements of Articles 15.2 and 15.3 are examined.

1. Protection of Traditional Knowledge

Conceptual and Implementation Issues

Different alternatives have been proposed to deal with indigenous/traditional knowledge or some components thereof. This is the case, for instance, regarding proposals relating to "tribal" or "communal" or "community intellectual rights",[10] and "traditional resource rights".[11]

---

10. Berhan and Egziabher, 1996, p. 38A Model of *sui generis* national legislation that would give communities property-like rights over their collective knowledge was developed by the Third World Network (Community Intellectual Rights Act) in 1994.
11. Posey and Dutfield, 1996.

Draft Article 15.2(a) of the revised International Undertaking requires measures for the protection of "traditional knowledge" but, in view of the scope and purpose of the Undertaking, it only refers to knowledge "relevant to plant genetic resources for food and agriculture". Thus, Article 15.2 is narrower in scope than Article 8(j) of the CBD, and would not apply, for instance, to knowledge relating to medicinal or industrial uses of plant genetic resources. Under this approach, the issue of protection of traditional knowledge may be circumscribed to knowledge incorporated in farmers' varieties ("landraces") and certain associated knowledge (e.g. specific cultivation practices).

The development of a *sui generis* regime for the protection of farmers' varieties becomes, in this context, one of the possible components of Farmers' Rights. This issue, as mentioned above, has received considerable attention in the literature, though little progress has been made in terms of actually implementing that kind of protection.

The establishment of a *sui generis* regime poses, in fact, complex conceptual and practical issues. On the conceptual level, it is not clear whether the protection of farmers' varieties under an IPRs system would have any positive impact on their conservation or stimulate breeding activity, and whether protection would serve the purpose of strengthening the rights of communities and traditional farmers over their resources.[12] There may be more appropriate non-IPR methods of protecting such varieties, for instance, via access legislation or a misappropriation regime as discussed below.

On the other hand, the impact of protecting farmers' varieties under an IPRs-system will vary according to the nature and characteristics of the national seed supply system in a particular country. Moreover, seed supply arrangements may be crop-specific. Hence, IPRs can play a different role depending on the crop at stake.[13]

12. IPGRI, 1999, p. 16.

13. These differences had been, in fact, recognized by the UPOV Convention until its revision in 1991. Member-countries were allowed, under UPOV 1978, to decide on which crops PBRs would be applicable. Article 4 made it obligatory to protect a minimum of 24 genus or species within eight years of the entry into force of the Convention in a member-country (Article 4.3).

If it were deemed that an IPRs-type of protection for farmers' varieties were desirable, a number of issues would need to be addressed:

Definition of Subject Matter (What is Protected?)

The delimitation of the subject matter is a critical and complex issue, since traditional agriculture does not conserve specific genotypes or populations, but rather a total complex of genetic diversity in evolution and flux. Such agriculture uses and manages genetic diversity in a dynamic system of continuous change and adaptation. Farmers' varieties are continuously replaced, introgressed and introduced to new environments and new selection pressures.[14]

Although modern techniques (molecular markers) facilitate a detailed description of the heritable material of plants and populations, it is apparently extremely difficult (if not impossible) to define individual landraces, which continuously evolve. In any case, a system of protection should be based (as in the case of breeders' rights) on the material existence of an identifiable variety.

Requirements in Order to Grant Protection

What level of novelty, if any, would be required in order to grant protection? One specific problem posed by farmers' varieties is that most of them have been in actual use for a considerable time, and therefore they can not be deemed "new" as required, for instance, under PBRs legislation.

Since farmers' varieties are more heterogeneous than varieties produced through classical breeding, the "uniformity" and "stability" requirements provided for under PBRs would not be suitable in most cases. A possible approach may be to define minimum genetic distances with regard to the composition of varieties with overlapping claims, or to define a maximum level of genotypes that can be shared by the two varieties.

Who is the Title-holder?

This question as to who is the title-holder is likely to be

14. Hardon, 1997, p. 46.

one of the main problems to be faced in efforts to make Farmer's Rights effective. The collective nature of innovations or creative works is not, *per se,* an obstacle to the recognition of protection.[15] The problem is that farmers' varieties generally have no single origin and they are the result of the interaction of multiple farmers, often in different regions or countries. Possible approaches to this problem may include one or more of the following options.

Possible Right-holders of Farmers' Rights

- Informal plant breeders from developing countries,
- Landowners where PGRFA are conserved and developed, if different from plant breeders,
- Farmers located in the centers of diversity of PGRs,
- Indigenous and rural communities,
- Individual farmers, where identifiable,
- Traditional small farmers, and
- National States.

The researcher advocates the recognition of Farmers' Rights as *collective* rights, that is, as rights that belong to communities or groups of farmers and not to individuals or to States. Another possible option is that the rights be administered by a State-sponsored or other kind of organization on behalf of farmers. For instance, a royalty could be charged at the national level on traded seed and the funds collected, administered and distributed by such an organization.[16]

Territorial Validity of Right

Patents and breeders' rights are territorial rights, in the sense that they are only valid in those countries where

15. See, for example, the UNESCO Model Law on Folklore.
16. Collective entities for the collection and administration of authors rights are common in the field of copyright and related rights. See WIPO, 1990.

registration has been obtained.[17] An important problem for a *sui generis* system is the spreading of landraces in several countries. If protection is restricted to a national jurisdiction, the varieties protected there could be in the public domain elsewhere. In order to ensure cross-border protection, similar substantive rules should be adopted by other countries unilaterally or on the basis of bilateral or plurilateral agreements.[18]

How would the System Operate?

Issues such as examination and registration should be carefully analysed, as well as the costs involved in the operation of a system of protection. The registration of the varieties as a condition for protection, though advisable in order to attain some degree of certainty, may pose a very heavy, often insurmountable, burden on farmers, especially the poorest. It would also require the establishment of new public functions, with their associated costs.

Enforceability

The availability of rights is useless if the system cannot be actually enforced. This depends on how easy it is or not to cheat; on the existence of preventive measures and remedies; and, above all, on the capacity to monitor and support the costs of administrative and judicial procedures. Given the essentially variable nature of farmers' varieties and the fact that providers and users thereof may be located in different countries, enforcement problems may be very substantial.

Duration

Another very important issue is that of determining the duration of protection for an intrinsically evolving material for

17. This is a major difference with copyrights, which do not require registration and have an almost universal validity by virtue of the application of international conventions.
18. The review of the TRIPs Agreement may provide an opportunity to develop a *sui generis* system with an international reach. However, this is unlikely to happen in the near future.

which, in addition, the date of "creation" cannot be established?

Compensation

As noted in respect of other aspects of the implementation of Farmers' Rights, various options exist in connection with the type of compensation to be granted. Such compensation may be based on funds generated from different sources as laid down below.

Possible Funding for Compensation

- Royalties on seed sales,
- Taxes on seed sales,
- Collection fees (for materials held *in-situ*), and
- Access fees (for materials held *ex-situ*).

The definition of the possible forms of compensation needs to take into account complex issues raised by the calculation thereof and by the allocation of funds to different farmers, groups or communities. Since many PGRs have been developed by different groups/communities, including in several countries, determining the "credit" of each group/community may be extremely difficult, if not impossible.

Moreover, the economic benefits derived from the commercial exploitation of germplasm provided by traditional farmers' may be difficult to estimate and "tax" and this may be insufficient to "really solve the problems of rural communities in terms of their economic needs, employment and management of natural resources. Royalties will be minor in comparison to what will go to the people who are engaged in the production and sale of seeds".[19]

Another issue that may require consideration is the use to be given to the funds received, if any, on the basis of Farmers' Rights. Should such funds be applied to conservation/development activities, or could the beneficiaries individual or collective freely dispose of them as they wished? It would seem that the latter solution should apply if decision-making

19. Shankar, 1996, pp. 171-72.

by farmers is to be reinforced, unless it is too difficult to identify the group that should receive the compensation.

In any case, in designing a new system of protection adequate consideration should be given to the expected benefits and costs for society, as well as the direct costs to be borne by the government.

Possible Approaches : (1) A Dual System

As noted above, a crucial issue in the establishment of a *sui generis* regime would be the definition of the protected subject matter. Article 27.3b of the TRIPs Agreement requires the protection of "plant varieties", but does not provide (as in the case of inventions) a definition thereof. Therefore, national laws have ample room to determine what is to be deemed a plant "variety" for the purposes of protection. There have been lengthy discussions on the concept of "plant variety", particularly in the framework of UPOV. The scientific notion does not necessarily coincide with the legal concept. The law may require certain characteristics for a *protected* variety that may not be essential for a scientific definition.

One option may be to distinguish different levels of protection depending upon the degree to which the uniformity and stability standards are met. Thus, varieties which meet such standards may be subject to rights broader than those applicable to varieties essentially characterized by their heterogeneity and variability. As mentioned, these are the features that confer great value on farmers' varieties as a source of germplasm for agricultural use.

A *sui generis* regime may, thus, provide for a *dual* system of protection,[20] which includes both "modern" as well as farmers' varieties. Under an UPOV-like legislation,[21] the requirements would include novelty, distinctness, uniformity and stability. For other cases (farmers' varieties) the

20. In Switzerland, for instance, a register for groupings of cereals that do not meet the ordinary homogeneity requirements has been established.
21. UPOV, 1978 provides a model for legislation that is more flexible and adaptable to the needs of developing countries than UPOV, 1991.

requirements may be less stringent and be limited, for instance, to sufficient identification and distinctness.

The inclusion of farmers' varieties as a protectable subject matter would imply a radical departure from existing IPRs regimes. One of the major difficulties in dealing with such varieties, however, is their essentially variable nature. The definition of the subject matter and, consequently, the enforcement of rights become more difficult and complex than in cases where uniformity and stability are present.

Nevertheless, the subject matter of protection under IPRs law need not always be defined with precision for the acquisition of the relevant rights. Thus, trade secrets are protectable without description and registration. It is a matter of proving in each individual case whether or not there has been infringement.

It may be convenient to make it clear, in any case, that protection should be granted with respect to a variety as such and that, therefore, it would not extend to any constituent of the plants, including their genetic information, nor to specific characteristics of the plants or of the harvested materials. In some jurisdictions, patents have been accepted on the basis of characteristics or functional specifications,[22] a possibility that a *sui generis* regime should clearly prevent.

In the case of farmers' varieties, the creation of the variety is generally a collective endeavour and, therefore, the rights should not be granted to individuals, but to the community that has developed and used the variety. Of course, the collective nature of these rights, and the dissemination of farmers' varieties in different areas or communities, may create controversies about the entitlement to the respective rights. This situation is not essentially different, however, from cases in which two or more persons or firms claim to have developed a given piece of technology or information. Co-ownership is also a possibility.

An important aspect of a *sui generis* regime relating to plant varieties would be the scope of the rights conferred on titleholders. In most cases, IPRs grant exclusive rights, that is, the faculty to prevent third parties from exploiting the

22. Correa, 1994.

protected subject matter. Some modalities of IPRs, however, do not entail exclusivity, but other types of rights. Even the TRIPs Agreement does not require the granting of exclusive rights in a number of instances, such as with respect to undisclosed information.

In the case of farmers' varieties, national legislation may recognize a "remuneration right", that is, an entitlement to receive compensation in all cases of use of a protected variety for propagating purposes outside the respective farming community or communities. This formulation would amount, in practice, to an open licensing system whereunder any interested party may utilize the protected variety for planting or multiplication, against a payment in favour of the titleholders. Consideration should also be given to the *status* of any derivatives of farmers' varieties, including essentially derived varieties, and the remuneration if any to be paid for these.

Possible Approaches: (2) A Misappropriation Prevention Regime

Another possible way of protecting farmers' varieties would be through a regime that aims to prevent the misappropriation of such varieties. This type of regime would not imply the establishment of any form of monopolization that could contradict farmers' practices and values, but the legal faculty to prevent multiplication or commercialization of propagating materials acquired in a manner that is contrary to the applicable rules on collection, transfer and use of germplasm.

Thus, national legislation may establish that no intellectual property rights shall be conferred with respect to farmers' varieties. In the case of infringement of this rule, the conferred title should be declared void. A delicate problem to be addressed is the extent to which derivatives from such varieties, particularly essentially derived varieties, should be also excluded from IPRs protection, or subject to the control of the original suppliers of the varieties.

If such a regime were established, national laws would be free to determine the means to prevent misappropriation, including criminal and civil remedies, and how to empower communities for the exercise and enforcement of their rights. Protection would not be subject under the proposed scheme—like as in the case of trade secrets—to any kind of registration. Protection would last for as long as the conditions that justify it subsist. Given the collective nature of these rights and that farmers communities generally lack a legal personality, a possible mechanism for enforcement may be to establish an "ombdusman" empowered with the right to act on behalf of the communities so as to enforce their rights.

Some of the main features of such a regime as proposed, are the following:

- it would recognize the informal, collective and cumulative systems of innovation of local and indigenous communities and farmers;
- no novelty, inventiveness or secrecy would be required;
- there would be no arbitrary time limit for protection;
- the conferred rights would be "non-monopolistic" and would not hinder the non-commercial use and exchange of germplasm within and among communities;
- no registration, and therefore, administrative machinery, would be necessary;
- it would not oblige farmers or communities' members to keep secrecy or change their traditional practices;
- since no monopolies would be recognized, possession of the same knowledge by different communities would be perfectly legitimate; and
- the rights against infringers would arise when a variety has been acquired in a manner contrary to certain rules, such as national access legislation or other accepted practices on the collection of germplasm.

2. Benefit-sharing

The FAO Resolution 5/89 introduced the concept of "benefit-sharing" as one of the *components* of Farmers' Rights. This concept was incorporated later in Article 15 of the CBD and given a broader scope. This article applies in relation to "the results of research and development and the benefits arising from the commercial and other utilization of all kinds of genetic resources". The CBD also added that such sharing should be "upon mutually agreed terms".

The fair and equitable sharing of benefits is a major goal of the CBD. It is also an important element in the International Undertaking. The draft text on Article 14 which was agreed (with a number of remaining brackets) by the Contact Group at its First Inter-sessional Meeting (Rome, 20-24 September 1999) provides that the benefit-sharing within the Multilateral System that is to be established will take place through the transfer of technology, capacity building and the exchange of information. Differences still exist on whether funding and a fair and equitable sharing of the results of R and D and of commercial exploitation of PGRFA would be included (Article 14.2, Document CGRFA/CG-1/99/TXT).

The same draft provision states that the benefits arising from the use of PGRFA should flow "directly or indirectly, to farmers in all countries, particularly in developing countries and countries with economies in transition who conserve and sustainably utilize PGRFA". However, it is not agreed whether such flows should "primarily" benefit such farmers or only "*inter alia*".

In April 2000 further discussion took place in the Contact Group on the monetary dimension of benefit-sharing and the following text was developed:

14.2 (d) Sharing of [monetary] benefits on commercialization

(i) [Parties agree, under the Multilateral System, to [share]/[promote] commercial benefit[s][-sharing] through measures that involve the private sector in activities identified under Article 14 of the International Undertaking through partnerships in research and technology development];

(ii) [Whenever the use of PGRFA accessed under the Multilateral System results in a product protected by patents, or any form of commercial protection that

> restricts further access to the genetic material involved for research and plant breeding, parties agree that a fixed share of royalties shall be paid into a mechanism to be decided by the Governing Body as a contribution to the implementation of agreed plans and programmes as established in accordance with Article 16.]

At this stage of the negotiation of the International Undertaking it is still uncertain how this issue will be finally solved, and the extent to which farmers will participate in benefits-sharing at the international level. As indicated above, however, one of the elements of Farmers' Rights to be realized at the *national* level, in accordance with draft Article 15.2(b), relates to benefit-sharing.

National governments may implement such sharing through a variety of modalities. One option is to include specific provisions in *access legislation,* as appropriate. Benefit sharing may also be implemented through farmers' access to funds arising from taxes or levies associated with trade in seeds, or through other charges imposed on breeders that benefit from farmers' contributions. This latter approach may be based on a general contribution (for instance, registration fees imposed on all breeders), or on payments associated with the specific use by a breeder of materials for which the contribution of traditional farmers may be determined and valued.

For this purpose, national patent, PBRs and seed laws may establish the obligation to reveal the source of a genetic material used for the creation of a new variety and, if appropriate in the particular case, to prove that the applicant has complied with rules relating to access and sharing of benefits. This type of requirement ("certificate of origin"), would not be inconsistent with the TRIPs Agreement, which does not limit the States rights to make the grant of a patent conditional on complying with certain obligations (such as the payment of a registration fee).

Whichever approach is followed, national governments should carefully examine the costs and benefits of any policy to be implemented and, in particular, of its likely impact on farmers, breeders and consumers. For example, taxes, or levies applied on seeds are likely to increase the prices charged to farmers, who may or may not transfer this extra cost to consumers, depending on market structure and conditions and regulatory requirements.

3. Participation of Farmers in Decision-making

One of the components of Farmers' Rights, according to draft Article 15.2(c) would be "the right to participate in making decisions" at the national level "on matters related to the conservation and sustainable use" of PGRFA.

This right, which would benefit "the local and indigenous communities and farmers", should be recognized, according to Article 15.2, "as appropriate" and subject to "national legislation". This means that national governments have considerable scope to determine the extent of such right.

The importance of ensuring the participation of local, indigenous and farming communities in decision-making concerning PGRFA has been stressed in various fora. In particular, the Draft UN Declaration on the Rights of Indigenous Peoples developed by the Working Group on Indigenous Populations recognizes the communities' rights to political and legal autonomy and the rights of indigenous peoples over cultural and genetic resources as follows:

> "Indigenous peoples are entitled to the recognition of full ownership, control and protection of their cultural and intellectual rights. . . . They have the right to special measures to control, develop and protect their sciences, technologies and cultural manifestations, including human and other genetic resources, seeds, medicines, knowledge of the properties of fauna and flora, oral traditions, literatures, designs and visual and performing arts" (Article 29).

Some national laws have begun to incorporate these principles. In the Philippines, the *Indigenous Peoples Rights Act* contains a broad recognition on community rights. Access legislation adopted in some countries also provides for some form of participation in relation to the collection of genetic materials. In accordance with the Philippines Executive Order No. 247, for instance, the rights of indigenous and local communities must be taken into account with regard to informed consent procedures.

The relationship between indigenous peoples and national governments is, however, problematic in many countries:

> "Some indigenous peoples understand themselves to be a nation within a nation or a nation whose peoples cross the borders of two or more nations. Some governments consider themselves to be the sole and entirely sufficient voice of all the peoples within their sovereign territory".[23]

The realization of Farmers' Rights in relation to farmers' participation in decision-making will be dependent, in the last instance, upon the nature of the relations between local, indigenous and farming communities, on the one hand, and national governments, on the other hand. A wide range of scenarios can be considered in this regard. Some tension may be expected between the exercise of such a right and the operation of a multilateral system, which requires a free flow of the germplasm in question. In any case, the formal recognition of Farmers' Rights in the International Undertaking would certainly constitute an important step towards the reaffirmation of farmers' and communities' rights to take decisions that essentially concern the kind of farming system that they wish to keep as an integral part of their culture and lifestyles.

4. The Right to Save, Sell and Exchange Seeds

As indicated above, farmers' rights with regard to saving, selling and exchanging seed is a controversial issue. One view is that farmers should be freed from any restriction with regard to the use and disposition of seeds, including those protected under IPRs. This view is not shared, however, by those who believe that the unrestricted use of IPRs-protected materials by farmers will erode the incentives to commercial breeding and create a threat to future world food security .

---

23. The Crucible II Group, 2000, p. 77.

As indicated above, a clear distinction must be made according to the types of materials involved. There can be no objection to the idea that one of the components of the Farmers' Rights should be the right to reuse *non-protected* seeds and to commercialize their own produce.

However, the distribution of non-protected farmers' varieties may be restricted by the relevant *national seed legislation,* which in many countries imposes constraints, based on agronomic considerations, aiming at ensuring the dissemination of adequate and safe seeds. It does not seem reasonable to think that this type of regulation pertaining to seeds could be overridden by a general concept of Farmers' Rights, but measures may be adopted in order not to unduly prevent farmer-based exchanges.

The implementation of this aspect of Farmers' Rights needs to distinguish between the various kinds of materials that may be involved in farmers' practices and the role of IPRs.

Farmers' Varieties

There is no doubt that farmers can use, exchange, sell or otherwise dispose of the varieties that they have developed and which are not subject to third parties' IPRs. In fact, farmers' varieties ("landraces") are today outside the IPRs system. They are within the "public domain". Hence, the farmer that has developed such varieties cannot be prevented from any action relating to them. At the same time, he/she has no legal faculty to prevent others from using or reproducing such varieties; this is precisely one of the problems that some proposals for *sui generis* protection aim to address.

Farmers' Own Produce

Similarly, farmers are free to dispose of their own produce, whether it has been obtained from their own varieties or with varieties protected by IPRs (unless this right is curtailed by contractual obligations imposed by seed distributors). In this sense, the recognition of the right to dispose of the "farm produce" as proposed, for instance, in the Indian law on PBRs, does not mean any significant concession to farmers, since they legally already enjoy the right to sell it.

Protected Varieties

The situation may be substantially different, however, in relation to the sale or other forms of distribution of seeds for propagating purposes, when such seeds are protected by third parties' IPRs. Though PBRs legislation has generally admitted an exception for the reuse of protected seeds in the farmers' own exploitation ("farmers' privilege"), it has normally prevented acts that may lead to further propagation without the consent of the PBRs titleholder.

The scope of the "farmers' privilege" varies in different national laws. Under UPOV 1978, most countries allowed such privilege in broad terms. The 1991 revision of UPOV has narrowed the scope for such exception, which can be established under national law, within reasonable limits and safeguarding the legitimate interests of the breeder (Article 15.2).

Since UPOV 1991, national laws have tended to restrict the scope of the farmers privilege to different degrees, both in developed and in developing countries. Thus, the European Community Plant Variety Rights (Council Regulation EC No. 2100/94) limits the "farmers' exception" to certain species and requires the payment of an "equitable remuneration" to the breeder for planting-back protected seeds, except in the case of "small farmers" (Article 14.2 and 14.3). In Brazil, law No. 9456 (1997) has established that such exception does not apply in relation to sugarcane. It only benefits small farmers, who can provide or exchange seeds on a non-commercial basis with other small farmers. In sum, PBRs provide some room for the farmers' practice of saving seed, but the recent legislative trend has been to restrict the room available for following such practice. Under product patent protection the restriction on such practice is straightforward and stronger than under PBRs. In principle, the patent owner may prevent such practice or require additional payment for the reuse of seeds.

Some options that would reconcile IPRs with the farmers' right to save, sell and exchange IPRs *protected* materials may be considered, such as the following:

1. To distinguish different groupings of farmers with regard to the planting-back of protected material, on

the basis of volume of output, size of landholdings, species concerned, etc. Thus, a broad farmers' exception may be granted to "primarily-subsistence farmers", or to "small" farmers who customarily reuse seed because they lack access to or financial resources for new seed every growing season. Large farmers in the commercial sector may be subject instead to other, more stringent, rules.

2. To exempt exchanges of seed that take place within the same community or with neighbours, and between farming communities.
3. To allow certain sales of seeds as propagating materials, for instance, those that take place within the farmers' customary market area.

All these activities may be important to maintain genetic diversity and enhance local plant breeding. Those activities under (2) and (3) may be seen, however, as a threat to PBRs and inconsistent with obligations under UPOV (where this convention is applicable), if such activities were not really an expression of traditional practices and were just used as a means to circumvent PBRs.[24]

5. Other Promotional Measures

As mentioned, the agreed draft Article 15.2 is merely illustrative; it indicates only some of the measures that States could take for the protection and promotion of Farmers' Rights, but it does not exclude other measures. Some promotional measures that may be adopted at the national level are as follows:

Measures that may be undertaken for the promotion of Farmers' Rights at the national level.

- Support of conservation and development of PGRFA by traditional farmers,
- Research,

24. The Crucible II Group, 2000, p. 99.

- Training,
- Integration of traditional and modern knowledge,
- Technical assistance and training,
- Transfer of technology,
- Improvement of access to credit, and
- Participation of farmers, e.g. via prior consent for access to PGRFA.

As shown above, there is a wide range of possibilities for promoting the realization of Farmers' Rights. Of course, any promotional measure would imply costs that many developing countries will not be in a position to bear. The development of international cooperation may be essential to implement promotional policies effectively.

Several interesting experiences made in a number of developing countries, offer possible approaches to be followed elsewhere, including the following examples:[25]

- Participatory plant breeding.[26]
- Agroecological-based natural resource management for low-income farmers.[27]
- Reintroducing farmers' varieties to replace modern varieties and reduce the vulnerability created by genetic uniformity (for example, experience with rice cultivation in the Henwal Valley, India).[28]
- Farmer-centred research and extension with a view to combining the knowledge and research capabilities of local farmers with those of R and D organizations (for example, centres for propagation in the region of Moramanga, Madagascar).[29]
- Low-External-Input Sustainable Agricultural Practices based on participatory development and support of farmers' experimentation (for example,

25. See also Srivastava, Jitendra, Smith, Nigel and Forno, 1998.
26. Eyzaguirre and Iwanaga, 1996; Smith, Weltzein, Meitzner and Sperling, 2000.
27. Altieri and von der Weid, 2000.
28. Singh, 1999, p. 12.
29. Tucker, 1999, p. 106.

experiences in northern Ghana, Andean valleys and Indian Deccan Plateau).[30]

The concept of Farmers' Rights, first introduced by the FAO in 1989, has been reaffirmed in a number of international instruments and is gaining growing recognition in some proposed national laws and regulations. Efforts to win full acceptance of this concept and its implication have been at the very heart of the negotiations for the revision of the International Undertaking.

The progress made in defining and realizing Farmers' Rights since the concept was adopted, has been slow. There are complex conceptual and practical problems that need to be addressed, including the relationship with IPRs. Opinions diverge, Farmers' Rights can be regarded as a "non-IPRs mechanism", but, in fact, the rationale for the recognition of Farmers' Rights significantly differs from that applicable to IPRs. The clarification of such rationale seems essential in order to characterize and define the content of Farmers' Rights. Equity, conservation, and the preservation of farmers' traditional practices, provide sound justifications for the establishment of such Rights.

Farmers' Rights may be seen as a moral recognition of farmers' past and present contributions to making agriculture sustainable. However, they can also play a significant role as concrete *instruments* to protect and promote traditional farming activities and communities' culture and lifestyles. To this end, important issues need to be clarified in relation to the scope, content, title-holders, duration and other aspects of such Rights.

The discussions and several proposals made in the context of the revision of the International Undertaking have contributed to the identification of the nature of certain actions that may be taken at the national level in order to implement Farmers' Rights. The possible scope and characteristics of such measures need to be further developed so as to provide more concrete guidelines to governments on how best to comply with their responsibilities in this field.

30. ILEIA, 1999, p. 5.

The preliminary consensus reached on a draft of Article 15 of the International Undertaking, has been an important step towards the definition of Farmers' Rights as a component of national policies. That Article also provides possible elements for the realization of those rights, while leaving considerable room for national governments to determine how to implement them through protective and promotional measures. Though this may lead to very different ways of approaching the matter, it also ensures that each country can adapt the concept to its own reality and needs.

There is still considerable work to be done to ensure that Farmers' Rights are recognized in practice. This will require, *inter alia*, capacity building, training, transfer of technology and a fair reward for farmers' contributions. Though the issues which are pending are important and complex there seems to be a gradual movement from the realm of ideas towards the design of such measures that can be realized in practice and which supports and promotes farmers' activities in the conservation and improvement of plant genetic resources for food and agriculture.

APPENDIX I

ARTICLE 15 : FARMERS' RIGHTS

(Article 15 as negotiated during the Eighth Regular Session of the Commission, April 1999)

15.1 : The Parties recognized the enormous contribution that the local and indigenous communities and farmers of all regions of the world, particularly those in the centres of origin and crop diversity, have made and will continue to make for the conservation and development of plant genetic resources which constitute the basis of food and agriculture production throughout the world.

15.2 : The Parties agree that the responsibility for realizing Farmers' Rights, as they relate to Plant Genetic Resources for Food and Agriculture, rests with national governments. In accordance with their needs and priorities, each Party should, as appropriate, and subject to its national legislation, take measures to protect and promote Farmers' Rights, including:

(a) protection of traditional knowledge relevant to plant genetic resources for food and agriculture;

(b) the right to equitably participate in sharing benefits arising from the utilization of plant genetic resources for food and agriculture;

(c) the right to participate in making decisions, at the national level, on matters related to the conservation and sustainable use of plant genetic resources for food and agriculture.

15.3 : Nothing in this Article shall be interpreted to limit any rights that farmers have to save, use, exchange and sell farm-saved seed/propagating material; subject to national law and as appropriate.

Document CGRFA-8/99.

APPENDIX II

FAO RESOLUTION 5/89 ON FARMERS' RIGHTS

The Conference,

Recognizing that:

(a) plant genetic resources are a common heritage of mankind to be preserved, and to be freely available for use, for the benefit of present and future generations,
(b) full advantage can be derived from plant genetic resources through an effective programme of plant breeding, and that, while most such resources, in the form of wild plants and old landraces, are to be found in developing countries, training and facilities for plant survey and identification, and plant breeding, are insufficient, or even not available in many of those countries, and
(c) plant genetic resources are indispensable for the genetic improvement of cultivated plants, but have been insufficiently explored, and in danger of erosion and loss.

Considering that:

(a) in the history of mankind, unnumbered generations of farmers have conserved, improved and made available plant genetic resources,
(b) the majority of these plant genetic resources come from developing countries, the contribution of whose farmers has not been sufficiently recognized or rewarded,

(c) the farmers, especially those in developing countries, should benefit fully from the improved and increased use of the natural resources they have preserved, and

(d) there is a need to continue the conservation (*in-situ* and *ex-situ*), development and use of the plant genetic resources in all countries, and to strengthen the capabilities of developing countries in these areas.

Endorses the concept of Farmers' Rights (Farmers' Rights mean rights arising from the past, present and future contributions of farmers in conserving, improving, and making available plant genetic resources, particularly those in the centres of origin/diversity. These rights are vested in the International Community, as trustee for present and future generations of farmers, for the purpose of ensuring full benefits to farmers, and supporting the continuation of their contributions, as well as the attainment of the overall purposes of the International Undertaking) in order to:

(a) ensure that the need for conservation is globally recognized and that sufficient funds for these purposes will be available;

(b) assist farmers and farming communities, in all regions of the world, but especially in the areas of origin/diversity of plant genetic resources, and

(c) allow farmers, their communities, and countries in all regions, to participate fully in the benefits derived, at present and in the future, from the improved use of plant genetic resources, through plant breeding and other scientific methods.

List of Cases

Canada, *Harvard College* v. *Canada (Commissioner of Patents)*, Supreme Court of Canada, Judgment of 5 December 2002, (2002) 4 *SCR* 45.

Canada, *Monsanto Canada Inc* v. *Schmeiser*, Supreme Court of Canada, Judgment of 21 May 2004, (2004) *SCC* 34.

European Court of Justice, *Netherlands* v. *European Parliament*, European Court of Justice, Judgment of 9 October 2001 (Case C377/98), [2001] 3 *CMLR* 49 (ECJ).

European Court of Justice, *Windsurfing Chiemsee* v. *Huber*, Cases C-108/97, C-109/97, Judgment of the European Court of Justice, 4 May 1999, [1999] ECR 1-2779.

European Patent Office, *Ciba-Geigy/Propagating Material*, European Patent Office Technical Board of Appeal, 26 July 1983 (T 49/83).

European Patent Office, *Lubrizoll Hybrid Plants* European Patent Office Technical Board of Appeal, 10 November 1988 (T 320/87).

European Patent Office, *Plant Genetic Systems* v. *Greenpeace*, European Patent Office, Technical Board of Appeal, 21 February 1995 (T 356/93).

European Patent Office, *Transgenic Plant/Novartis II*, European Patent Office Enlarged Board of Appeal, 20 December 1999 (G 0001/98), [2000] *EPOR* 303

European Patent Office, Opposition Division, Decision Revoking the European Patent 0436257, 10 May 2000.

GATT, *Tuna/Dolphin/Restrictions on Imports of Tuna (Mexico* v. *USA),* GATT Panel Report, 30 Int'l *Leg Mat* 1594 (1991).

GATT, *Tuna/Dolphin II, Restrictions on Imports of Tuna (EEC and Netherlands* v. *USA),* GATT Panel Report, 33 *Ml Leg Mat* 839 (1994).

India, *Scotch Whisky Association* v. *Pravara Sahakar Shakar Karkhana* AIR 1992 Bom 294.

India, *Chandra Bhavan Boarding and Lodging vs. The State of Mysore,* 1970, 2.S.C.R. 600.

India, *Dimminaco A.G.* v. *Controller of Patents Designs and Trade marks* (Unreported—for details of Case See IPR Bulletin Vol. 8, No. 7-9. July-September 2002, published by Technology Information, Forecasting and Assessment Council (TIFAC). Department of Science and Technology, New Delhi.

International Court of Justice, *Case Concerning the Gabcikovo-Nagymaros Project (Hungary/Slovakia),* International Court of Justice, Judgment, 25 September 1997, *ICJ Reports 1997,* at p. 7.

International Court of Justice, Separate Opinion of Vice-President Weeramantry, *Case Concerning the 'Gabdkovo-Nagymaros Project (Hungary/Slovakia)',* International Court of Justice, Judgment, 25 September 1997, *ICJ Reports 1997,* at p. 88.

South Africa, *The Pharmaceutical Manufacturers' Association of South Africa et al* v. *The President of the Republic of South Africa et al,* Notice of Motion, High Court of South Africa (Transvaal Provincial Division), 18 February 1998.

South Africa, *The Pharmaceutical Manufacturers' Association of South Africa et. al.* v. *The President of the Republic of South Africa et. al.* Joint Statement of Understanding (2001).

United Kingdom, *Cambridge Water Company* v. *Eastern Countries Leather,* House of Lords, 9 December 1993, [1994] 2 *AC* 264.

United States, *Asgrow Seed Company* v. *Denny Winterboer and Becky Winterboer, dba Deebees,* Supreme Court of the United States, 18 January 1995, 115 *USP Q* 788.

United States, *Cameron Septic Tank Co.* v. *Village of Saratoga Springs, 159 Fed.453,462(2nd Cir. 1908).*

United States, *Charles-Pfizer & Co. Inc* v. *Olin MathiesonChem. Corp. 155 U.S.P.Q. 139, 151 D.N.J 1967).*

United States, *City of Milwaukee* v. *Activated Sludge, Inc. 69 F 2d 577, 582-583 (7th Cir. 1934).*

United States, *Diamond* v. *Chakrabarty,* Supreme Court of the United States, 16 June 1980, 100 *S Ct* 2208.

United States, *Diamond* v. *Diehr, 209 U. S.P.Q 1.9 (1981).*

United States, *Diamond vs. Chakrabarty (1980) SC, 447 US 303.*

United States, *Douglas* v. *United States, 181 U.S.P.Q. 170, 176-77 (Ct.Cl. 1974).*

United States, *Embrex Inc.* v. *Service Engineering Corp. 216 F 3d 1343, 1352-53 (Fed. Cir. 2000).*

United States, *Ethicon* v. *United States Surgical Corporation,* United States District Court—D Connecticut, 9 September 1996, 937 *F Supp* 1015.

United States, *Ex parte Brian, 118 U.S.P.Q. 242, 245 (POBA 1958).*

United States, *Ex parte Hibberd,* Patent and Trademark Office Board of Patent Appeals and Interferences, 18 September 1985, 227 *USPQ* 443.

United States, *Ex parte Allen 2 U.S.P.Q 2d 1425, 1427 (BPAI 1987).*

United States, *Funk Bros. Seed Co.* v. *Kalo Inoculant Co, 233 U.S. 127 (1948) (First Bio tech case to reach the sc).*

United States, *Hurlbut* v. *Schillinger,* Supreme Court of the United States, 22 April 1889, 9 *S Ct* 584.

United States, *In re Bergy, 596 F.2d 952, 988 (CCPA 1979)*

United States, *In re Jolly, 367 F 2d 906 (CCPA 1967).*

United States, *In re Kirk, 376 F 2d 936 (CCPA 1967).*

United States, *J. E. M. Ag Supply Inc.* v. *Pioneer Hi- Bred Intl Inc 534 US 124 (2001).*

United States, *JEM AG Supply* v. *Pioneer Hi-Bred International,* Supreme Court of the United States, 10 December 2001, 122 *S Ct* 593.

United States, *Merck & Co Inc* v. *Chase Chemical Co. 155 U.S.P.Q. 139, 151 (D.N.J 1967).*

United States, *Monsanto* v. *Kamp,* United States District Court—District of Columbia, 15 June 1967, 269 *F Supp* 818.

United States, *Monsanto* v. *McFarling,* United States Court of Appeals—Federal Circuit, 23 August 2002, 302 *F 3d* 1291.

United States, *National Basketball Association* v. *Motorola Inc. 105 F 3d 841 (2nd Cir. 1997).*

United States, *Parker* v. *Flook 437 U.S. 584 (1978).*

United States, *SEC* v. *Sterling Precision Corp. 393F 2d 214, 220 (2d Cir. 1968).*

United States, *Shields* v. *Halliburton,* United States Court of Appeals—Fifth Circuit, 19 February 1982, 667 F 2d 1232.

United States, *TVA* v. *Hill, 437 US 153, 178 (1978).*

United States, *United States* v. *Dubilier Condenser Corp. 289 U.S. 178 (1933).*

United States, *Yoder Bros. Inc.* v. *California-Florida Plant Corp. 537 F 2d 1347 (5th Cir 1976).*

WTO, *Canada—Patent Protection of Pharmaceutical Products,* Report of the Panel 17 March 2000, WTO Doc WT/DS114/R.

WTO, *European Communities—Conditions for the Granting of Tariff Preferences to Developing Countries,* Report of the Panel, 28 October 2003, WTO Doc WT/DS246/R.

WTO, *European Communities—Conditions for the Granting of Tariff Preferences to Developing Countries,* Report of the Appellate Body, 18 March 2004, WTO Doc WT/DS246/AB/R.

WTO, *European Communities—Measures Affecting the Approval and Marketing of Biotech Products* Request for Consultations by the United States, WTO Doc WT/DS291/1 (2003).

WTO, *India—Patent Protection for Pharmaceutical and Agricultural Chemical Products (US complaint),* Report of the Panel, 5 September 1997, WTO Doc WT/DS50/R.

WTO, *India—Patent Protection for Pharmaceutical and Agricultural Chemical Products (US complaint),* Report of the Appellate Body, 19 December 1997, WTO Doc WT/DS 50/AB/R.

WTO, *India—Patent Protection for Pharmaceutical and Agricultural Chemical Products (EC complaint)*, Report of the Panel, 24 August 1998, WTO Doc WT/DS79/R.

WTO, *United States—Import Prohibition of Certain Shrimp and Shrimp Products (India, Malaysia, Pakistan and Thailand* v. *USA)*, Report of the Appellate Body, 12 October 1998, WTO Doc WT/DS58/AB/R.

WTO, *United States—Sections 301-310 of the Trade Act of 1974*, Report of the Panel, 8 November 1999, WTO Doc WT/DS152/R (1999).

Bibliography

Books

Agarwal, Bina, *A Field of Ones Own—Gender and Land Rights in South Asia* (Cambridge: Cambridge University Press, 1994).

Barnum, Susan R. *Biotechnology—An Introduction* (Belmont, CA: Wadsworth, 1998).

Baslar, Kemal. *The Concept of the Common Heritage of Mankind in International Law* (The Hague: Kluwer Law International, 1998).

Benedick, Richard Elliot. *Ozone Diplomacy—New Directions in Safeguarding the Planet* (Cambridge, Mass: Harvard University Press, enlarged ed. 1998).

Berhan, Tewolde and Egziabher (1996), *"A case of community rights"*, in Tilahun, S. and Sue, E (Editors). 1996. *The movement for collective intellectual rights*, The Institute for Sustainable Foundation/The Gaia Foundation, Addis Ababa.

Berkes, Fikret ed. *Common Property Resources—Ecology and Community-based Sustainable Development* (London: Belhaven Press, 1989).

Brush, Stephen (2000), *Genes in the field. On-Farm Conservation of Crop Diversity*, IPGRI/IDRC/LEWIS PUBLISHERS, Rome, Ottawa, Boca Raton.

C.S. Venkata Ratnam, *'Giobalisition and Labour-Management Relation : Dynamics of Change'*, (Response Books, New Dèlhi, 2001).

Carreau, Dominique. *Droit International* (Paris: Pedone, 7th ed., 2001).

Carvalho, Nuno Pires De. *The TRIPS Regime of Patent Rights* (London: Kluwer Law International, 2002).

Cassese, Antonio. *International Law in a Divided World* (Oxford: Clarendon, 1986).

Churchill, R.R., and A.V. Lowe. *The Law of the Sea* (Manchester: Manchester University Press, 3rd ed., 1999).

Clavier, Jean-Pierre. *Les categories de la propriite intellectuelle a I'e'preuve des creations genttiques* (Paris: L'Harmattan, 1998).

Conway, Gordon R, and Edward, B. Barbier. *After the Green Revolution—Sustainable Agriculture for Development* (London: Earthscan, 1990).

Cornish, W.R. *Intellectual Property: Patents, Copyright, Trade Marks, and Allied Rights* (London: Sweet and Maxwell, 5th ed. 2003).

Correa, Carlos (2000), *"In situ conservation and intellectual property rights"*, Brush, Stephen (Ed.), *GENES in the FIELD. On-Farm Conservation of Crop Diversity*, IPGRI/ IDRC/LEWIS PUBLISHERS, Boca Raton, Ottawa and Rome.

Cot, Jean-Pierre, and Alain Pellet eds. *La charte des Nations Unies—Commentaire article par article* (Paris: Economica, 2nd ed., 1991).

Crucible Group. *People, Plants, and Patents—The Impacts of Intellectual Property on Biodiversity, Conservation, Trade, and Rural Society* (Ottawa: International Development Research Centre, 1994).

Crucible II Group. *Seeding Solutions—Volume 2* (Ottawa: International Development Research Centre, 2001).

Cullet, Philippe. *Differential Treatment in International Environmental Law* (Aldershot: Ashgate, 2003).

Dutfield, Graham (1999), *Intellectual Property Rights, Trade and Biodiversity: The Case of Seeds and Plant Varieties*, Oxford University, Oxford.

Dutfield, Graham. *Intellectual Property Rights and the Life Cycle Industries* (Aldershot: Ashgate, 2003).

Dutfield, Graham. *Intellectual Property, Biogenetic Resources and Traditional Knowledge* (London: Earthscan, 2004).

Esquinas Alcazar, José (1996), "The realisation of Farmers' Rights", in *Agrobiodiversity and Farmers' Rights*, Madras: Swaminathan Research Foundation, No. 14.

Evenson, R., Gollin, D. and Santaniello, V. (Editors) (1998), *Agricultural Values of Plant Genetic Resources*, FAO/CEIS/CABI Publishing, Wallingford.

Eyzaguirre, P. and Iwanaga, M. (1996), *Participatory Plant Breeding*, IDRC/FAO/CPRO-DLO-CGN/IPGRI, Rome.

FAO (1994a), *"Revision of the International Undertaking. Issues for consideration in stage II: access to plant genetic resources, and Farmers' Rights"*, CPGR-Ex 1/94/5, Rome.

FAO (1994b), *"Revision of the International Undertaking: Analysis of some technical, economic and legal aspects for consideration in Stage II"*, CPGR-Ex 1/94/5 Supp., Rome.

FAO (1998), *The state of the world's plant genetic resources for food and agriculture*, Rome.

FAO, *The State of Food Insecurity in the World*, 2002 (2002).

Fidler, David P., *International Law and Infectious Diseases* (Oxford: Oxford University Pressm, 1999).

Fracesca Grifo and Joshua Rosenthal (des.) *Biodiversity and Human Health*. Washington DC, Island Press, 1997.

Friedman, W: *'Law in a Changing Society'*, Sweet and Maxwell Ltd. U.K, First Indian reprint, 2nd edn., 1996.

Gervais, Daniel, *The TRIPS Agreement—Drafting History and Analysis* (London: Sweet and Maxwell, 2003).

Girsberger, Martin (1999), *Biodiversity and the Concept of Farmers' Rights in International Law. Factual Background and Legal Analysis*, Peter Lang, Berne.

Glachant, M. and Leveque F. (1993), *L'enjeu des resources genetiques vegetales*, Les Editions de l'Environnement, Paris.

Gollin, D. (1998), "Valuing Farmers' Rights", Evenson, R.; Gollin, D. and Santaniello, V. (eds.) (1998), *Agricultural Values of Plant Genetic Resources*, FAO/CEIS/CABI Publishing, Wallingford.

GRAIN (2000), *For a full review of TRIPs 27.3(b). An update on where developing countries stand with the push to patent life at WTO*, Barcelona.

Grifo, Francesca, *The Origins of Prescription Drugs*. Washington DC, Island Press, 1997.

Gupta, A., 1998, *Postcolonial developments: Agriculture in the making of modern India*, Durham: Duke University Press

Gupta, A., 1998 *Postcolonial developments : Agriculture in the making of modern India.*

Gutterman, Alan (1997), *Innovation and competition policy*, Kluwer Law International, London.

Hanna, Susan S., Carl Folke and Karl-Goran Maler eds. *Rights to Nature—Ecological, Economic, Cultural, and Political Principles of Institutions for the Environment* (Washington, DC: Island Press, 1996).

Hannikainen, Lauri, *Peremptory Norms (Jus Cogens) in International Law—Historical Development, Criteria, Present Status* (Helsinki: Finnish Lawyers' Publishing, 1989).

Hardon, Jaap (1997), *"Ethical Issues in Plant Breeding, Biotechnology and Conservation: A Review"*, Ethics and Equity in Conservation and use of Genetic Resources for Sustainable Food Security, IPGRI, Rome.

Holyoak, Jon and Torremans, Paul, *Intellectual Property Law*. Second Edition, Butterworths, London, 1998.

Indian Council of Agricultural Research, 1990, *Plant Breeders' Rights in India.*

IPGRI (1999), *Key Questions for decision-makers, Protection of plant varieties under the WTO Agreement on Trade-Related Aspects of Intellectual Property Rights*, Rome.

Iver, P. Cooper, *Biotechnology and the Law*, Volume 1, p. 1.1 Pub-West Group, 1999.

Jean, Dre'ze and Amartya Sen, *'India Economic Development and Social Opportunity'* (Oxford University Press, Delhi, 1995).

Kate, Kerry Ten, and Sarah, A. Laird, *The Commercial Use of Biodiversity—Access to Genetic Resources and Benefit-Sharing* (London: Earthscan, 1999).

Larid, S., Alexaides, M. Bannister, K. Posey, D., Publication of Biodiversity Reaserch Results and the Flow of Knowledge.

In: Larid, Sarah (ed.), 2002. *'Biodiversity and Traditional Knowledge, Equitable Partnerships in Practice'*. WWF, RBGKew and UNESCO. Earthscan Publications Ltd. London.

Leskien, Dan and Flitner, Michael (1997), *"Intellectual Property Rights and Plant Genetic Resources: Options for a Sui Generis System"*, PGRI, Issues in Genetic Resources, No. 6.

Lewinski, Silke von ed. *Indigenous Heritage and Intellectual Property—Genetic Resources, Traditional Knowledge, and Folklore* (The Hague: Kluwer Law International, 2004).

Louwaars, N.P. and Marrewijk, G.A. (1996), *Seed Supply Systems in Developing Countries*, Technical Centre for Agricultural and Rural Cooperation, Wageningen Agricultural University, The Netherlands.

Louwaars, Niels P. (1996), *Expansion of Intellectual Property Rights Systems in Plants: Issues—Related with Plant Genetic Resources*, CPRO-DLO, Wageningen (The Netherlands).

M.S. Swaminathan, *'Agro-bio-diversity and Farmers' Rights'*, Proceeding of Technical Consultation of Implementation Framework For Farmers' Right, MSSRF, Madras (1996).

Mahbub ul Haq, Human Development Centre, *Human Development in South Asia, 2002—Agriculture and Rural Development* (Karachi: Oxford University Press, 2003).

Marin, Patricia Lucia Cantuaria, *Providing Protection for Plant Genetic Resources—Patents, Sui Generis Systems, and Biopartnerships* (London: Kluwer Law International, 2002).

Matthews, Duncan, *Globalising Intellectual Property Rights—The TRIPS Agreement* (London: Routledge, 2002), May, Christopher, *A Global Political Economy of Intellectual Property Rights —The New Enclosures?* (London: Routledge, 2000).

Mooney, P. (1996), "View point of Non-Governmental Organizations", in *Agrobiodiversity and Farmers' Rights*, Swaminathan Research Foundation, Madras.

Narayanan, P., *Patent Law* (Calçutta: Eastern Law House, 3rd ed., 1998).

Neeson, J.M., *Commoners—Common Right, Enclosure and Social Change in England, 1700-1820* (Cambridge: Cambridge University Press, 1993).

National Research Council (1993), *Agricultural Crop Issues and Policies: Managing Global Genetic Resources*, National Academy Press, Washington, D.C.

Oppenheim, L., *International Law—A Treatise* (Ronald F. Roxburgh ed., 3rd ed. Vol. 1, London: Longmans, 1920).

Ostrom, Elinor, *Governing the Commons—The Evolution of Institutions for Collective Action* (Cambridge: Cambridge University Press, 1990).

Otten, Adrian (1996), "Viewpoint of the WTO", in *Agrobiodiversity and Farmers' Rights*, Swaminathan Research Foundation, Madras.

Pauwelyn, Joost, *Conflict of Norms in Public International Law—How WTO Law Relates to Other Rules of International Law* (Cambridge: Cambridge University Press, 2003).

Posey, D.A. and G. Dutfield (1996), *Beyond Intellectual Property: tTraditional Resource Rights for Indigenous Peoples and Local Communities*, International Development Research Centre, Ottawa.

Prabuddha Ganguli, *Intellectaual Property Rights, Unleashing the Knowledge Economy*, Tata McGraw-Hill, New Delhi.

R.N. Basu, *'Biotechnology and Bioethics'*, Pub. Paschimbanga Bignan Mancha, Kolkatta.

Radin, Margaret Jane, *Contested Commodities* (Cambridge, Mass: Harvard University Press, 1996.

RAFI (Rural Advancement Foundation) (1994), *Conserving Indigenous Knowledge: Integrating Two Systems of Innovations*, Ottawa.

Roscoe Pound, *'An Introduction to Philosophy of Law'*, Universal Book Traders, Delhi, First Indian Reprint, 1995.

Rostow, W., The Stages of Economic Growth—A Non-Communist Manifesto, (Cambridge: Cambridge University Press, 3rd ed., 1990).

Ruiz, Manuel, *Protection sui generis de Econiomientos Indigenous en la Anazonia*, Corporation Andina de Fomento, Parlamento Andino y Socieded Peruna de Derecho Ambiental. Lima, 2002.

Schrijver, Nico, *Sovereignty Over Natural Resources—Balancing Rights and Duties* (Cambridge: Cambridge University Press, 1997).

Sharma, Rita, and Thomas, T. Poleman, *The New Economics of India's Green Revolution—Income and Employment Diffusion in Uttar Pradesh* (New Delhi: Vikas, 1994).

Shaw, Malcolm N., *International Law* (Cambridge: Cambridge University Press, 5th ed., 2003).

Shiva, Vandana, *The Violence of the Green Revolution* (London: Zed, 1991).

Singh, Abha Lakshmi, and Shahab Fazal, *Agriculture and Rural Development* (New Delhi: BR Publishing, 1998).

Singh, Bhupinder, and Need Mahanti, eds. *Intellectual Property Rights and the Tribals* (New Delhi: Inter-India Publications, 1997).

Singh, Gurdev and S.R. Asokan, *Seed Replacement Rates—Performance and Problems* (New Delhi: Oxford and IBH, 1994).

Ten Kate, Kerry and Larid, Sarah, *The Commercial Use of Biodiversity, Access to Genetic Resources and Benefit Sharing*, Earthscan Publications Ltd. London, 1999.

The Crucible II Group (2000), *Seeding Solutions. Vol. 1: Policy Options for Genetic Resources: People, Plants, and Patents Revisited*, IDRC, IPGRI, Dag Hammarskjöld Foundation, Rome.

Thomas, Jeffrey S. and Michael A. Meyer, *The New Rules of Global Trade—A Guide to the World Trade Organisation* (Scarborough, Ont: Carswell, 1997).

Tobin, B., *'Biodiversity and Traditional Knowledge. Equitable Partnerships in Practice.'* WWF, RBGKew and UNESCO. Earthscan Publications Ltd. London.

Toebes, Brigit C.A., *The Right to Health as a Human Right in International Law* (Antwerpen: Intersentia, 1999).

Upendra Baxi, *'Environmental Teaching and Research In Universities'*, in Association of Indian Universities (ed.) Environmental Challenges and the Universities, 44 (1994)

Vandana Shiva, 1996, *'Future of Our Seeds, Future of Our Farmers: Agricultural Bio-diversity, Intellectual Property and Farmers' Rights'*. *Pub:* Research Foundation for Science Technology and Ecology, New Delhi.

Vogel, Joseph. *El Acrtel de la Biodiverside. Transformacion de los Conocimientos Tradicinales en Secretos Comerciales*. SAN REM, Ecociencia, USAID. Quito, 2000.

Vogler, John. *The Global Commons—A Regime Analysis* (Chichester: John Wiley, 1995).

Watal, Jayashree. *Intellectual Property Rights in the WTO and Developing Countries* (New Delhi: Oxford University Press, 2001).

WIPO (1990), *Collective Administration of Copyright and Neighboring Rights*, Geneva.

World Commission on Environment and Development, *Our Common Future* (Oxford: Oxford University Press, 1987).

Wright, B. (1998), "Intellectual Property and Farmers' Rights", Evenson, R.; Gollin, D. and Santaniello, V. (eds.) (1998), *Agricultural Values of Plant genetic Resources*, FAO/CEIS/ CABI Publishing, Wallingford.

Articles

Altieri, Miguel and von der Weid, Jean-Marc (2000), "*Prospects for Agro-ecologically-based Natural-resource Management for Low-income Farmers in the 21st Century*" (paper presented at the GFAR Conference 2000, Dresden, May 21-23).

Aoki, K. (1988), *Neocoloninaism, Anticommons Property, and Biopiracy in the not-so-brave New World Order of International Intellectual Property Protection*. Indiana Journal of Global Legal Studies, 6, 11-58.

B.S. Chimni, *'The Philosophy of Patents : Strong Regime Unjustified'*, Journal for Scientific and Industrial Research. Volume 52, 1993, pp. 234-39.

Blochinger Karen (2000): *'A Variety of Interpretations of Plant Variety'*, CASRIP Newsletter, Vol. 7, Issue I.

Brush, Stephen (1994), *Providing Farmers' Rights Through In Situ Conservation of Crop Genetic Resources*, A Report to the Commission on Plant Genetic Resources, University of California.

Burch, B.K. *et al.* 2000. Divergent Incentives to Protect Intellectual Property: A Political Economy Analysis of North-south Welfare. *Journal of World Intellectual Property,* 3 (2), March.

Carl F. Jordon, *Genetic Engineering, the Farm Crisis and World Hunger,* 52, BIOSCIENCE 523, 526 (2002).

CIEL, *'Comments on Improving Identification of Prior Art. Recommendations on traditional Knowledge Relating to Biological Diversity'*—Submitted to the United States Patents and Trademark Office, August, 1999.

Correa, Carlos (1994), *"Sovereignty and Property Rights over Plant Genetic Resources",* Report to the Commission on Plant Genetic Resources, FAO, Rome.

Correa, Carlos (1999), *"Access to Plant Genetic Resources and Intellectual Property Rights",* FAO, Commission on Genetic Resources for Food and Agriculture, Background Study Paper No. 8.

Correa, Carlos (2000), *"In-situ Conservation and Intellectual Property Rights",* Brush, Stephen (Ed.), *GENES in the FIELD. On-Farm Conservation of Crop Diversity,* IPGRI/ IDRC/LEWIS PUBLISHERS, Boca Raton, Ottawa and Rome.

Dr. A. Jayagovind : *'From Order to Chaos—Some Reflections on International Economic Order',* Paper Presented at 'The Commonwealth Legal Education Association Conference' on 'Economic Policies, Human Rights and The Legal Order' held at Bangalore on 4-6-1993.

Dr. Raghunandha Reddy: *'A Market Driven Economy : The Constitutional Drift and Paradigm Shift',* Indian Bar Review, Vol. 29(2) 2002, p. 63.

Dr. V. Shiva and Afsar H. Jafri, The Need for Genuine *Sui Generis* Law to defend Farmers Rights as Traditional breeders : (From Internet- www.vshiva.net).

Economic and Social Commission for Asia and the Pacific, Institutional Capacity building to Deal with the Implications of TRIPs for Industrial and Technological Development: Case Study of India, 2001.

Erratt and Sechley (2000). *"The European Biotechnology Directive and the Patentability of Higher Life Forms"*, Canadian Biotechnology, 2000.

Esquinas Alcazar, José (1996), *"The Realisation of Farmers Rights"*, in *Agrobiodiversity and Farmers' Rights,* Madras: Swaminathan Research Foundation, No. 14. (Konark, 1996).

Eyzaguirre, P. and Iwanaga, M. (1996), *Participatory Plant Breeding,* IDRC/FAO/CPRO-DLO-CGN/IPGRI, Rome.

Fowler, Cary (2000), *"Implementing Access and Benefit-sharing Procedures under the Convention on Biological Diversity: The dilemma of Crop Genetic Resources and their Origins"*, GFAR Conference, 2000, Dresden, May 21-23.

Fugile, Klotz and Gill 1995: *New Group Varities AREI Update No. 14,* US Department of Agriculture Economics Research Service.

Gadgil, M. *et. al., New Meaning for Old Knowledge: The People's Biodiversity Registers Programme,* Submitted as an invited paper for Ecological Applications.

Genet (2001): *'Monsanto and Syngenta Monopolise Key Gene Marker Technologies'*, May 16.

Girsberger, Martin A., *'Transparency Measures under Patent Law regarding Genetic Resources and Traditional Knowledge—Disclosure of Source and Evidence of Prior Informed Consent and Benefit-Sharing'*, 7/4/World Intell Prop 451 (2004).

Gopalakrishnan, N.S. (2001), *An 'Effective' Sui Generis Law to Protect Plant Varieties and Farmers' Right in India—A Critique.* Journal of World Intellectual Property, January.

Greengrass, Barry, (1996), *"UPOV and Farmers' Rights"*, in *Agrobiodiversity and Farmers' Rights,* Swaminathan Research Foundation, Madras.

Harward, T. Markey, *'Patentibility of Animals in the US'*20 IIC, 372 (1987), p. 376.

Heller, M. and Eisenberg, R. (1998), *Can Patents Deter Innovation? The Anticommons in Biomedical Research.* Science 280.

Hirai Akimitsu (2001), *'Biotechnology and Legal Protection: Current Issues'*, CASRIP Newsletter, Winter.

Hiraki Yusuke (2000), *'Problems Regarding the Patentability of Genomics and Scope of Protection in of ESTs in Japan'*, CASRIP Newsletter, Winter.

ILEIA (1999), *"ILEIA Collaborative Research Programme"*, LEISA, ILEIA Newsletter, September.

Intellectual Needs and Property and "Traditional Knowledge Holders". WIPO Report on Fact Finding Missions on Intellectual Property and "Traditional Knowledge" (1998-1999) Geneva, April, 2001.

Jordan, Carl F., *'Genetic Engineering, the Farm Crisis and World Hunger,* 52 Bioscience 523 (2002).

Kadilal, S. (1997), *Subject-matter Imperialism? Biodiversity, Foreign Prior Art and the Neem Patent Controversy,* Idea: The Journal of Law and Techology, 37.

Klotz, Fugile and Pray (1995), *'Private sector Agricultural Research Expiernce in the US 1960-92'*. Staff paper No. AGF SI 525, US Department of Agriculture Economics Research Service, October.

Lori Ann Thrupp, *'Linking Agriculture Biodiversity and Food Security: The Valuable Role of Agrobiodiversity for Sustainable Agriculture'*, 76, INTERNATIONAL AFFAIRS 265, 268 (2000).

M.D. Nair, *'Amendment to Patent Act : Option Under TRIPS'*, The Hindu Daily, March 8, 2001 p. BS-3.

M.R. Agosin *et al.*, *"Developing Countries And the Uruguay Round : An Evaluation And Issues For The 'Future'"*, in United Nations Conference on Trade and Development Report (1995).

M.S. Swaminathan, *'Agro-biodiversity and Farmers' Rights'* Proceeding of Technical Consultation of Implementation Framework For Farmers' Right, MSSRF Madras (1996).

M.S. Swaminathan, *Ethics and Equity in the Use and Collection of Plant Genetic Resources: Some Issues and Approaches in International Plant Genetic Resources Institute,* Ethics and Equity in Conservation and Use of Genetic Resources and Sustainable Food Security, 7 (1997).

Malcolm Gladwell, *'Are Scientists Wrong to Patent Genes'*—Span April/May 1996, 54P-52.

Md. Zafar Mahfooz Nomani, *'Laws And Flaws Relating to Conservation of Biological Diversity : A Kaleidoscopic View'*, (2002), 2, The Company Law Journal, pp. 17-22.

Md. Zafar Mahfooz Nomani, *'The Human Right To Environment In India : Legal precepts and Judicial Doctrines in Critical Perspective'* (2000), 5, The Asia Pacific Journal of Environmental Law, 113-34.

Md. Zafar Mahfooz Noomani, *'Environment Agriculture and Challenges of Biopiracy: A Blue Print of Indian Sui-Generis Legal Order'*. Paper presented in the International Conference on Environment Agriculture and Poverty, Department of Geography, A.M.U., Aligarh, (March 4-5, 2001).

Patricia, A. Rac, *'Patentibility of Living Subject Matter'*. 10, CIPR 4 (1993).

Petit, Michel, Fowler, Cary, Collins, Wanda, Correa, Carlos and Thornström, Carl-Gustaf; (2000), *"Why Governments Can't Make Policy. The Case of Plant Genetic Resources in the International Arena"*, CGIAR draft.

Pharmalicensing (2001): *'Plants and IP Protection'*, May 2.

Philipe Cullet, *'Revision of the TRIPS Agreement Concerning The Protection of Plant Varieties : Lessons From India Concerning The Development of A Sui Generis System'*, 2(4) The Journal of World Intellectual Property, 625 (1999).

Philippe Cullet, 'Bill On IPRs I : *'Bio-Diversity Legislation Reflects India's Obligation'*, The Hindu Daily, Feb. 22, 2001, B5-4.

Philippe Cullet, *'Bill On IPRs III : Bio-Diversity Bill Insists on Sovereign Right's*, The Hindu Daily, March 8, 2001, B5-4.

Phillip Cullet, *'Bill On IPRs IV : Concerns With Proposed Law'*, The Hindu Daily, March 15, 2001 p. BS-4.

Phillippe Cullet, *'Intellectual Property Rights: For An Alternative Patent Regime'*, *xvi(21)* The Frontline Magazine, 91(1999).

R.A. Mashelkar, *"Intellectual Property Rights and Third World"*, Journal of Intellectual Property Rights, Vol. 7, July, 2002.

Rajeev Dhavan and Maya Prabhu, *'Patent Monopolies and Free Trade : Basic Conttradiction in Dunkel Draft'*, XXXVII (2), The Journal of Indian Law Institute, 195-208, (1995).

Rajeev Dhavan, Lindsay Harris and Gopal Jain, *'Power Without Responsibility : On Aspect of the Indian Patents Legislation'*, XXXIII (1), The Journal of Indian Law Institute, 2-6 (1991).

Ramanna, A., 2001, *India's Policy on IPRs and Agriculture: Relevance of FAO's New International Treaty*. Economic and Political Weekly, Commentary, 36(51), December 22.

Ramaswami and Ballasundaram, *'Impact of GATT on Indian Agricultural Biodiversity and Patenting Issues'*—Productivity, Volume 42, 3 October-December 2001.

Riley, Kenneth (1996), "Farmers' Rights, CGIAR and IPGRI", in *Agrobiodiversity and Farmers' Rights*, Swaminathan Research Foundation, Chennai.

Ruiz, Manuel, Analisis de la Decision 486 de Resources Geneticos y Conocimientors Tradicionales. Documento preparado para la Corporacion Andina de Fomento (version en brrador). Lima, 2002.

S. Biswasnathan, C. Parmar, *'A Biotechnology Story'*, Economic and Political Weekly, July 6th, 2002.

Sahai, S., 2000, *Farmer's Rights and Food Security*, Economic and Political Weekly, Commentary, March 11-17.

Seshia, S. (2001), *Plant Variety Protection and Farmers' Rights : Law-Making and Cultivation of Varietal Control* Economic and Political Weekly, July 6.

Shankar, Darshan (1996), *"Tribal and Rural Farmer-conservers"*, in *Agrobiodiversity and Farmers' Rights*, Swaminathan Research Foundation, Chennai.

Singh, Vir (1999), *"Traditional Agro-biodiversity Re-introduced by Farmers"*, *LEISA*, ILEIA Newsletter, Vol. 15, No. 3/4.

Smith, M., Weltzein, E., Meitzner, L. and L. Sperling (2000), *Technical and Institutional Issues in Participatory Plant Breeding from the Perspective of Formal Plant Breeding : A Global Analysis of Issues, Results, and Current Experience*, Working Document 3, PRGA Program, Cali, Colombia.

Srinivas, K Ravi, *'Interpreting Para 6: Deal on Patents and Access to Drugs'*, *38/38*, Economic and Political Weekly, 3975 (2003).

Srinivasan, C. (1996), "*Current Status of Plant Variety Protection in India*", in *Agrobiodiversity and Farmers' Rights*, Swaminathan Research Foundation, Madras.

Srinivasan, C.S., '*Concentration in Ownership of Plant Variety Rights: Some Implications for Developing Countries*', 28, Food Policy 519 (2003).

———, '*Exploring the Feasibility of Farmers' Rights*', 21/4, Dev Poly Rev 419 (2003).

——— (2004), *International Trends in Plant Variety Protection* in *Agrobiodiversity and Farmers' Rights*, Swaminathan Research Foundation, Madras.

Srinivasan, C.S., and Colin Thirtle, '*Understanding the Emergence of Terminator Technologies*', 12 J Int Dev, 1147 (2000).

Srivastava, Jitendra and Jaffee, Steven (1993), "*Best Practices for Moving Seed Technology, New approaches to doing business*", World Bank Technical Paper Number 213, Washington, D.C.

Srivastava, Suresh C., '*Geographical Indications and Legal Framework in India*, 38/38, Economic and Political Weekly, 4022 (2003).

Suman Sahai, '*Indian Patent Act and TRIPS*', *XXVIII*, The Economic and Political Weekly, 1495 (1993).

Swaminathan ed., *Agrobiodiversity and Farmers' Rights*, 77 (New Delhi: Konark, 1996).

Swaminathan, M.S. (1994), "*Reaching the Unreached : Dialogue 5 on Farmers' Rights*", *Methodologies for Recognizing the Role of Informal Innovation in the Conservation and Utilization of Plant Genetic Resources*. M.S. Swaminathan Research Fundation, January.

Swaminathan, M.S., '*Ethics and Equity in the Collection and Use of Plant Genetic Resources: Some Issues and Approaches*', in IPGRI, *Ethics and Equity in Conservation and Use of Genetic Resources for Sustainable Food Security*, 7 (Rome: International Plant Genetic Resources Institute, 1997).

Swanson, T. and Luxmoore, R. (1996), *Industrial Reliance upon Biodiversity: a Darwin Initiative Project*, DOE.

Swanson, T., D. Pearce and, R. Cervigni (1994), "*The Appropriation of the Benefits of Plant Genetic Resources for Agriculture: An Economic Analysis of the Alternative*

Mechanisms for Biodiversity Conservation", Report to the Commission on Plant Genetic Resources, Rome: FAO.

The Crubile II Group. *Seeding Solutions. Volume 1: Policy Options for Genetic Resources. People, Plants and Patents revised.* IDRC, IPGRI, and Dag Hammarskjold Foundation, Italy, 2000, p. 1.

Thrupp, Lori Ann. *'Linking Agricultural Biodiversity and Food Security: The Valuable Role of Agrobiodiversity for Sustainable Agriculture'*, 76 Int'lAff 265 (2000).

TIFAC, 1998, Database on Patent Applications filed in India.

Tucker, Terry (1999), *"Farmer-centered Research and Extension"*, CIIFAD, Annual Report 1998-99, Ithaca.

Tulatip Natural Resources. Culture Stories. ICONS CD ROM, 2002.

V. Shiva, *'Agricultural Biodiversity, Intellectual Property Rights and Farmers' Rights,'*, Economic and Political Weekly, June 22, 1996, p. 1622.

V.R., Krishna Iyer, *GATT, TRIPS and Patent Law*-I, The Hindu Daily : New Delhi Edition, Sept. 11, 2000, p. BS-4.

Venner, Raymond and Alston, Julian (1999), *"The Effects of the U.S. Plant Variety Protection Act on Wheat Genetic Improvement"*.

Weidlich, S., 1996. *The Discussion about Plant Breeders' Rights in India, ASA Paper*, CDG Carl Duisberg Gesellschaft.

Conventions, Declaration, Recommendations, Reports (Govt. and Pvt.) and Treaties

Agreement on Trade-Related Aspects of Intellectual Property Rights, Marrakech, 15 April 1994, *33 Inti Leg Mat* 1197 (1994).

Agreement Between the World Intellectual Property Organisation and the World Trade Organisation, Geneva, 22 December 1995.

Agreement Establishing the World Trade Organisation, Marrakesh, 15 April 1994, *33 Int'l Leg Mat* 1144 (1994).

Agreement for the Repression of False or Deceptive Indications of Source on Goods, Madrid, 14 April 1891.

Agreement on the Application of Sanitary and Phytosanitary Measures, Marrakesh, 15 April 1994, in World Trade Organisation, *The Legal 'Texts—The Results of the Uruguay Round of Multilateral Trade Negotiations* (Cambridge: Cambridge University Press, 1999).

Agreement Relating to the Implementation of Part XI of the United Nations Convention on the Law of the Sea of 10 December 1982, New York, 28 July 1994, 33 *Int'l Leg Mat* 1309 (1994).

Agreement to Revise the Bangui Agreement on the Creation of an African Intellectual Property Organisation of 2 March 1977, Bangui, 24 February 1999.

American Convention on Human Rights, San Jose, 22 November 1969, 9 *Int'l Leg Mat* 673 (1970).

Cartagena Protocol on Biosafety to the Convention on Biological Diversity, Montreal, 20 January 2000, 39 *Int'l Leg Mat* 1027 (2000).

Charter on Human and Peoples' Rights, Banjul, 19 January 1982, 21 *Int'l Leg Mat* 58 (1982).

Convention Establishing the World Intellectual Property Organisation, Stockholm, 14 July 1967.

Convention for the Protection of Industrial Property, Paris, 20 March 1883.

Convention for the Protection of Literary and Artistic Works, Berne, 9 September 1886.

Convention for the Safeguarding of the Intangible Cultural Heritage, UNESCO, Paris, 17 October 2003.

Convention on Access to Information, Public Participation in Decision-making and Access to Justice in Environmental Matters, Aarhus, 25 June 1998, 38 Int'l *Leg Mat* 517 (1999).

Convention on Biological Diversity, Rio de Janeiro, 5 June 1992, 31 *Int'l Leg Mat* 818 (1992).

Convention on Civil Liability for Damage Resulting from Activities Dangerous to the Environment, Lugano, 21 June 1993, 32 *Int'l Leg Mat* 1228 (1993).

Convention on Civil Liability for Nuclear Damage, Vienna, 21 May 1963 as amended by the Protocol of 12 September 1997.

Convention on International Trade in Endangered Species of Wild Fauna and Flora, Washington, 3 March 1973, 12 *Int'l Leg Mat* 1085 (1973).

Convention on Persistent Organic Pollutants, Stockholm, 23 May 2001, 55 *Int'l Leg Mat* 531 (2001).

Convention on the Conservation of Antarctic Marine Living Resources, Canberra, 20 May 1980, 19 *Int'l Leg Mat* 837 (1980).

Convention on the Grant of European Patents, Munich, 5 October 1973.

Convention on the Law of Treaties, Vienna, 23 May 1969, 8 *Int'l Leg Mat* 679 (1969).

Convention on Wetlands of International Importance Especially as Waterfowl Habitat, Ramsar, 2$_{m}$ February 1971, 11 *Int'l Leg Mat* 963 (1972).

Convention to Combat Desertification in Those Countries Experiencing Serious Drought and/or Desertification, Particularly in Africa, Paris, 17 June 1994, 33 *Int'l Leg Mat* 1328 (1994).

Framework Convention on Climate Change, New York, 9 May 1992, 31 *Int'l Leg Mat* 849 (1992).

General Agreement on Tariffs and Trade: Multilateral Trade Negotiations, Final Act Embodying the Results of the Uruguay Round of Trade Negotiations, Marrakesh, 15 April 1994.

Instrument for the Establishment of the Restructured Global Environment Facility, Geneva, 16 March 1994, 33 *Int'l Leg Mat* 1273 (1994).

International Convention for the Protection of New Varieties of Plants, Paris/Geneva, 2 December 1961, 23 October 1978 and 19 March 1991 [Geneva: UPOV Doc 221(E), 1996].

International Convention on Civil Liability for Oil Pollution Damage, London, 27 November 1992.

International Covenant on Civil and Political Rights, New York, 16 December 1966, 6 *Ml Leg Mat* 368 (1967).

International Covenant on Economic, Social and Cultural Rights, New York, 16 December 1966, 6 *Int'l Leg Mat* 360 (1967).

International Treaty on Plant Genetic Resources for Food and Agriculture, Rome, 3 November 2001.

International Tropical Timber Agreement, Geneva, 26 January 1994, 33 *Int'l Leg Mat* 1014 (1994).

Paris Convention for the Protection of Industrial Property, 20 March 1883, (as revised and amended).

Patent Cooperation Treaty, Washington, 19 June 1970, PCT Applicants Guide, 9 *Int'l Leg Mat* 978 (1970).

Patent Law Treaty, Geneva, 1 June 2000, WIPO Doc PT/DC/47.

Trademark Law Treaty, Geneva, 27 October 1994.

Treaty on the International Recognition of the Deposit of Micro-organisms for the Purposes of Patent Procedure, Budapest, 28 April 1977.

United Nations Convention on the Law of the Sea, Montego Bay, 10 December 1982, 21 *Int'l Leg Mat* 1261 (1982).

Convention on Biodiversity

Akwe¢: Kon Voluntary Guidelines for the Conduct of Cultural, Environmental and Social Impact Assessment Regarding Developments Proposed to Take Place on, or which are Likely to Impact on, Sacred Sites and on Lands and Waters Traditionally Occupied or Used by Indigenous and Local Communities, in Section H (Annex), Decision VII/16, Article 8(j) and Related Provisions, in Report of the Seventh Meeting of the Conference of the Parties to the Convention on Biological Diversity, UN Doc UNEP/CBD/COP/7/21 (2004).

Bonn Guidelines on Access to Genetic Resources and Fair and Equitable Sharing of the Benefits Arising out of their Utilisation, in Report of the Sixth Meeting of the Conference of the Parties to the Convention on Biological Diversity, UN Doc UNEP/CBD/COP/6/2G (2002).

Decision BS-I/8, Establishment of an Open-Ended Ad Hoc Working Group of Legal and Technical Experts on Liability and Redress in the Context of the Protocol, in Report of the First Meeting of the Conference of the Parties Serving as the Meeting of the Parties to the

Protocol on Biosafety, UN Doc UNEP/CBD/BS/COP-MOP/1/15 (2004).

Decision II/12, Intellectual Property Rights, in Report of the Second Meeting of the Conference of the Parties to the Convention on Biological Diversity, UN Doc UNEP/CBD/COP/2/19 (1995).

Decision III/11, Conservation and Sustainable Use of Agricultural Biological Diversity, in Report of the Third Meeting of Conference of the Parties to the Convention on Biological Diversity, UN Doc UNEP/CBD/COP/ 3/38 (1996).

Decision III/17, Intellectual Property Rights, in Report of the Third Meeting of the Conference of the Parties to the Convention on Biological Diversity, UN Doc UNEP/CBD/COP/3/38 (1997).

Decision III/8, Memorandum of Understanding between the Conference of the Parties to the Convention on Biological Diversity and the Council of the Global Environment Facility, in Report of the Third Meeting of Conference of the Parties to the Convention on Biological Diversity, UN Doc UNEP/CBD/COP/3/38 (1996).

Decision IV/9, Implementation of Article 8(j) and related provisions, in Decisions Adopted by the Conference of the Parties to the Convention on Biological Diversity at its Fourth Meeting, UN Doc UNEP/CBD/COP/4/27 (1998).

Decision VI/5, Agricultural Biological Diversity, in Report of the Sixth Meeting of the Conference of the Parties to the Convention on Biological Diversity, UN Doc UNEP/CBD/COP/6/20 (2002).

Decision VII/16, Article 8(j) and Related Provisions, in Report of the Seventh Meeting of the Conference of the Parties to the Convention on Biological Diversity, UN Doc UNEP/CBD/COP/7/21 (2004).

Decision VII/19, Access and Benefit-sharing as Related to Genetic Resources (Article 15), in Report of the Conference of the Parties to the Convention on Biological Diversity, Seventh Meeting, Doc UNEP/CBD/COP/7/21 (2004).

Programme of Work on Agricultural Biological Diversity, Conference of the Parties to the Convention on Biological Diversity, Fourth Meeting, UN Doc UNEP/CBD/COP/4/6 (1998).

Recommendations for the Conduct of Cultural, Environmental and Social Impact Assessments Regarding Developments Proposed to Take Place on, or which are Likely to Impact on, Sacred Sites and on Lands and Waters Traditionally Occupied or Used by Indigenous and Local Communities, in Annex II, Decision VI/10, Article 8(j) and Related Provisions, UN Doc UNEP/CBD/COP/6/20 (2002).

Terms of Reference for the Ad Hoc Open-Ended Working Group on Access and Benefit-Sharing, in Report of the Conference of the Parties to the Convention on Biological Diversity, Seventh Meeting, Doc UNEP/CBD/ COP/7/21, page 300 (2004).

Consultative Group on International Agricultural Research

CDC Statement to ICW 2000 on the Need to Resolve Outstanding Issues Concerning Intellectual Property Protection Relating to Plant Genetic Resources, CGIAR International Centres Week (2000).

Centres' Position Statement on Genetic Engineering (1998).

CGIAR Center Statements on Genetic Resources, Intellectual Property Rights, and Genetic Engineering.

Declaration and Plan of Action for Global Partnership in Agricultural Research, Global Forum on Agricultural Research at the Consultative Group on International Agricultural Research, International Centers Week, 31 October 1996.

International Plant Genetic Resources Institute, *Key Questions for Decision-makers—Protection of Plant Varieties under the WTO Agreement on Trade-Related Aspects of Intellectual Property Rights* (Rome: IPGRI, 1999).

Lucerne Declaration and Action Program, in Renewal of the CGIAR—Sustainable Agriculture for Food Security in Developing Countries—Ministerial-level Meeting—Summary of Proceedings and Decisions (1995).

Progress Report on IPRs Matters and Proposal for Review of Plant Breeding, Mid-Term Meeting, Beijing, CGIAR Doc MTM/99/20 (1999).

European Region

Amended Proposal for a European Parliament and Council Directive Approximating the Legal Arrangements for the Protection of Inventions by Utility Model, *OJ*, C 248E, 29/08/2000, p. 56.

Council Directive 98/44 on the Legal Protection of Biotechnological Inventions 1998, *OJ*, L 213/13.

Council of Europe—Parliamentary Assembly Recommendation 1425 (1999)—Biotechnology and Intellectual Property.

Council Regulation (EC) No. 2100/94 on Community Plant Variety Rights, 27 July 1994, *OJ*, L 227/1.

Council Regulation (EC) No. 2501/2001 of 10 December 2001 Applying a Scheme of Generalised Tariff Preferences for the Period from 1 January 2002 to 31 December 2004, *OJ*, L/346 (31 December 2001), p. 1.

Council Regulation (EC) No. 953/2003 of 26 May 2003 to Avoid Trade Diversion into the European Union of Certain Key Medicines, 26 May 2003, O/L 135/5, 3 June 2003.

Directive 2004/35/CE of the European Parliament and of the Council of 21 April 2004 on Environmental Liability with Regard to the Prevention and Remedying of Environmental Damage, *Official Journal*, L 143/56 (30 April 2004).

Directive 98/44/EC of the European Parliament and the Council of the European Union on the Legal Protection of Biotechnological Inventions, 6 July 1998, *OJ*, L 213.

FAO

Commission on Genetic Resources for Food and Agriculture, Possible Formulas for the Sharing of Benefits Based on Different Benefit-Indicators, Rome, 8th Session, 19-23 April 1999, Doc CGRFA-8/99/8.

Commission on Plant Genetic Resources, Revision of the International Undertaking—Analysis of Some Technical, Economic and Legal Aspects for Consideration in Stage II : Access to Plant Genetic Resources and Farmers' Rights, Doc CPGR-6/95/8 Supp (1995).

FAO (1994a), "Revision of the International Undertaking. Issues for Consideration in Stage II: Access to Plant Genetic Resources, and Farmers' Rights", CPGR-Ex1/94/5, Rome.

FAO (1994b), "Revision of the International Undertaking: Analysis of Some Technical, Economic and Legal Aspects for Consideration in Stage II", CPGR-Ex 1/94/5 Supp., Rome.

FAO (1998), *The State of the World's Plant Genetic Resources for Food and Agriculture*, Rome.

FAO, *Agricultural Biotechnology—Meeting the Needs of the Poor?* (Rome: FAO, 2004).

FAO, *The State of Food Insecurity in the World 2004* (Rome: FAO, 2004).

FAO, *World Agriculture—Towards 2015/2030* (London: Earthscan, 2003).

First Inter-sessional Meeting (Rome, 20-24 September 1999) Document CGRFA/CG-1/99/TXT.

International Undertaking for Plant Genetic Resource, Resolution 8/83, Report of the Conference of FAO, 22nd Session, Rome, 5-23 November 1983, Doc C83/REP.

Preliminary Draft International Code of Conduct on Plant Genetic Engineering as it Affects the Conservation and Utilisation of Plant Genetic Resources in Commission on Genetic Resources for Food and Agriculture, Towards a Code of Conduct for Plant Genetic Engineering as it Affects the Conservation and Utilisation of Plant Genetic Resources, 9th Session, Rome, 14-18 October 2002, Doc CGRFA-9/02/18/Annex.

Resolution 3/91, Report of the Conference of FAO, 26th Session, Rome, 9-27 November 1991, Doc C91/REP.

Resolution 4/89, Agreed Interpretation of the International Undertaking, Report of the Conference of FAO, 25th Session, Rome, 11-29 November 1989, Doc C89/REP.

Resolution 5/89, Farmers' Rights, Report of the Conference of FAO, 25th Session, Rome, 11-29 November 1989, Doc C89/REP.

Resolution 7/93, Revision of the International Undertaking on Plant Genetic Resources, Report of the Conference of FAO, 27th Session, Rome, 6-24 November 1993, Doc C93/REP.

Third Meeting of Commission I of the 30th Period of FAO Conference (Rome, 16 November 1999).

World Food Summit, Plan of Action, Rome, 17 November 1996.

United Nations

Agenda 21, in Report of the United Nations Conference on Environment and Development, Rio de Janeiro, 3-14 June 1992, UN Doc A/CONF 151/26/Rev 1 (Vol. 1), Annex II.

Commission on Human Rights, Resolution 2001/33, Access to Medication in the Context of Pandemics such as HIV/AIDS, 23 April 2001, UN Doc E/2001/23-E/CN 4/2001/167.

Committee on Economic, Social and Cultural Rights, General Comment No 3, 'The Nature of States Parties' Obligations (Art 2, para. 1 of the Covenant)', in Compilation of General Comments and General Recommendations Adopted by Human Rights Treaty Bodies, UN Doc HRI/GEN/1/Rev. 7.

Committee on Economic, Social and Cultural Rights, Draft General Comment No. 18, The Right of Everyone to Benefit from the Protection of the Moral and Material Interests Resulting from any Scientific, Literary or Artistic Production of which he is the Author, Article 15 (l)(c) of the International Covenant on Economic, Social and Cultural Rights.

Committee on Economic, Social and Cultural Rights, General Comment No. 12, The Right to Adequate Food (Art. 11), UN Doc. E/C.12/1999/5 (1999).

Committee on Economic, Social and Cultural Rights, General Comment No. 14. The Right to the Highest Attainable Standard of Health, UN Doc E/C 12/2000/4 (2000).

Committee on Economic, Social and Cultural Rights, Report on the Twenty-second, Twenty-third and Twenty-fourth Sessions, UN Doc E/2001/22-E/C 12/2000/21.

Committee on Economic, Social and Cultural Rights, Statement on Human Rights and Intellectual Property, November 2001, Annex XIII, Committee on Economic, Social and Cultural Rights Report on the Twenty-fifth, Twenty-sixth and Twenty-seventh Sessions, UN Doc E/ 2002/22-E/C 12/2001/17.

Declaration of Alma-Ata, 12 September 1978, in Report of the International Conference on Primary Health Care (Geneva: World Health Organisation, 1978).

Declaration of the United Nations Conference on the Human Environment, Stockholm, 16 June 1972, 11 *Int'l Leg Mat* 1416 (1972).

Declaration on the Right to Development, 4 December 1986, UN General Assembly Resolution 41/128, UN Doc A/ RES/41/53.

Draft Covenant on Economic, Social and Cultural Rights, Commission on Human Rights, Report of the 10th Session, ECOSOC, 18th Session, Supp 7, Doc E/2573—E/ CN 4/705 (1954).

Draft Declaration on the Rights of Indigenous Peoples, UN Sub-Commission on Prevention of Discrimination and Protection of Minorities, 46th Session, 1994, UN Doc E/ CN 4/Sub 2/1994/2/Add 1.

Draft International Covenant on Human Rights, Report of the 3rd Committee, UN Doc A/3764 (1957). Draft International Declaration of Human Rights—Mexico: Amendment to Article 25 of the Draft Declaration, UN Doc A/C 3/266 (1948).

Draft Resolution: The Role of Patents in the Transfer of Technology to Under-developed Countries, General Assembly, 2nd Committee, 16th Session, UN Doc A/C 2/ L 565 (1961).

General Assembly Resolution 2625 (XXV), Declaration on Principles of International Law Concerning Friendly Relations and Co-operation among States in Accordance with the Charter of the United Nations, 24 October 1970, 9 *Int'l Leg Mat* 1292 (1970).

General Assembly Resolution 3201 (S-VI), Declaration on the Establishment of a New International Economic Order, 1 May 1974, 13 *Int'l Leg Mat* 715 (1974).

General Assembly Resolution 1713 (XVI), The Role of Patents in the Transfer of Technology to Under-developed Countries, 19 December 1961.

General Assembly Resolution 1803 (XVII), Permanent Sovereignty over Natural Resources, 14 December 1962, 2 *Int'l Leg Mat* 223 (1963).

General Assembly Resolution 42/187, Report of the World Commission on Environment and Development, 11 December 1987, UN Doc A/RES/42/187.

General Assembly Resolution 47/191, Institutional Arrangements to Follow-up the United Nations Conference on Environment and Development, 22 December 1992, UN Doc A/RES/47/191.

General Assembly Resolution 55/2, United Nations Millennium Declaration, 18 September 2000, UN Doc A/RES/55/2.

General Assembly Resolution 58/1B, Scale of Assessments for the Apportionment of the Expenses of the United Nations, 23 December 2003, UN Doc A/RES/58/1B.

General Assembly Resolution S-18/3, Declaration on International Economic Cooperation, in particular the Revitalisation of Economic Growth and Development of the Developing Countries, 1 May 1990, UN Doc A/S-18/15.

International Law Commission, Draft Articles on the Responsibility of States for Internationally Wrongful Acts, Report on the Work of its Fifty-third Session, UN Doc A/56/10, p. 43 (2001).

Johannesburg Declaration on Sustainable Development, 4 September 2002, UN Doc A/CONF 199/20.

Non-Legally Binding Authoritative Statement of Principles for a Global Consensus on the Management, Conservation and Sustainable Development of all Types of Forests, Rio de Janeiro, 14 June 1992, 31 *Int'l Leg Mat* 881 (1992).

Report of the Third Session of the Commission on Human Rights, UN Doc E/800 (1948).

Rio Declaration on Environment and Development, 14 June 1992, UN Doc A/CONF 151/26/Rev 1 (Vol. 1), Annex I.

Role of Patents in the Transfer of Technology to Underdeveloped Countries, Report by the Secretary General, UN Doc E/3861-E/C 5/52/Rev 1 (1964).

Sub-Commission on the Promotion and Protection of Human Rights, Resolution 2000/7, Intellectual Property Rights and Human Rights, 17 August 2000, UN Doc E/CN 4/Sub 2/2000/7.

THE UNESCO Model Law on Folklore.

Third Committee Summary Record of Meetings, UN Doc A/C 3/SR 150 (1948).

Third Committee Summary Record of Meetings, UN Doc A/C 3/SR 151 (1948).

Third Committee Summary Record of Meetings, UN Doc A/C 3/SR 796 (1957).

Third Committee Summary Record of Meetings, UN Doc A/C 3/SR 797(1957).

Third Committee Summary Record of Meetings, UN Doc A/C 3/SR 798 (1957).

UN Charter, San Francisco, 26 June 1945.

UNCTAD, A Case Study of the Pharmaceutical Industry in India, in UNCTAD, *Transfer of Technology for Successful Integration into the Global Economy*, 87 (Geneva: UNCTAD, 2003).

UNCTAD, The Least Developed Countries Report 2004, UN Doc UNCTAD/LDC/2004 (2004).

UNCTAD, The Role of the Patents System in the Transfer of Technology to Developing Countries, UN Doc TD/B/AC 11/19 (1974).

UNDP, *Human Development Report* (New York: Oxford University Press, 2000, 2003, 2004).

Universal Declaration of Human Rights, 10 December 1948, UN General Assembly Resolution 217 (III) A, Official Records of the Third Session of the General Assembly, Part 1, 21 September-12 December 1948 (Resolutions).

World Health Assembly, HIV/AIDS: Confronting the Epidemic, Resolution WHA 53:14 (20 May 2000).

World Summit on Sustainable Development, Plan of Implementation, 4 September 2002, UN Doc A/CONF 199/20.

WIPO, WTO/GATT

Committee on Trade and Development—Special Session, Report to the WTO Doc TN/CTD/3 (2003).

Communication from India, WTO Doc IP/C/W/195 (2000).

Communication from Switzerland—Article 27.3(b), The Relationship between the TRIPS Agreement and the Convention on Biological Diversity, and the Protection of Traditional Knowledge, WTO Doc IP/C/W/400/Rev 1 (2003).

Composite Study on the Protection of Traditional Knowledge, Inter-governmental Committee on Intellectual Property and Genetic Resources, Traditional Knowledge and Folklore, Doc WIPO/GRTKF/IC/5/8 (2003).

Decision of the Council for TRIPS, Implementation of Article 66.2 of the TRIPS Agreement, 19 February 2003, WTO Doc IP/C/28.

Declaration on the TRIPS Agreement and Public Health, Ministerial Conference—Fourth Session, WTO Doc WT/MIN(01)/DEC/2 (2001).

Differential and More Favourable Treatment, Reciprocity and Fuller Participation of Developing Countries (Enabling Clause), Decision of the Contracting Parties, 28 November 1979, GATT Doc L/4903.

Doha Work Programme on Special and Differential Treatment and Outstanding Implementation Issues, Communication from Bangladesh (on behalf of the LDC Group), India, Indonesia, Mauritius (on behalf of the African Group) and

Trinidad and Tobago (on behalf of the ACP Group), 31 March 2004, WTO Doc WT/GC/W/528-TN/C/W/16.

Doha Work Programme, Decision of the General Council, 1 August 2004, WTO Doc WT/L/579.

Draft Substantive Patent Law Treaty, Standing Committee on the Law of Patents, 10th Session, Geneva, May 2004, WIPO Doc SCP/10/4.

Draft Technical Study on Disclosure Requirements Related to Genetic Resources and Traditional Knowledge, Intergovernmental Committee on Intellectual Property and Genetic Resources, Traditional Knowledge and Folklore, 5th Session, Doc WIPO/GRTKF/IC/5/10, WIPO/GRTKF/IC/2/6 (2003).

Extension of the Transition Period under Article 66.1 of the TRIPS Agreement for Least-Developed Country Members for Certain Obligations with respect to Pharmaceutical Products, Decision of the Council for TRIPS, 27 June 2002, WTO Doc IP/C/25.

General Council, Implementation of Paragraph 6 of the Doha Declaration on the TRIPS Agreement and Public Health, Decision of 30 August 2003, WTO Doc WT/L/540 (2003).

General Council, Generalised System of Preferences, Decision of the Contracting Parties, 25 June 1971, GATT Doc L/3545.

Implementation of Paragraph 6 of the Doha Declaration on the TRIPS Agreement and Public Health, Council for TRIPS, 16 December 2002, WTO Doc JOB(02)/217.

Implementation-Related Issues and Concerns, WTO Ministerial Conference, Fourth Session, Doha, November 2001, Doc WT/MIN (01)/17.

Intellectual Needs and Property and "Traditional knowledge" Holders. WIPO Report on Fact Finding Missions on Intellectual Property and "traditional knowledge" (1998-1999) Geneva, April 2001.

Inter-governmental Committee on Intellectual Property and Genetic Resources, Traditional Knowledge and Folklore, Overview of Activities and Outcomes of the Intergovernmental Committee, Doc WIPO/GRTKF/IC/5/12 (2003).

Least-Developed Country Members—Obligations under Article 70.9 of the TRIPS Agreement with Respect to Pharmaceutical Products, Decision of the General Council, 8 July 2002, WTO Doc WT/L/478.

Matters Concerning Intellectual Property and Genetic Resources, Traditional Knowledge and Folklore, WIPO General Assembly, 26th Session, Doc WO/GA/26/6 (2000).

Ministerial Declaration on the Uruguay Round, 20 September 1986, Multilateral Trade Negotiations, Doc MIN DEC.

Ministerial Declaration, WTO Ministerial Conference, Fourth Session, Doha, 14 November 2001, Doc WT/MIN(01)/DEC/1.

Proposal by Argentina and Brazil for the Establishment of a Development Agenda for WIPO, WIPO General Assembly, 31st (15th Extraordinary) Session, Doc WO/GA/31/11 (2004).

Review under Article 24.2 of the Application of the Provision of the Section of the TRIPS Agreement on Geographical Indications, WTO Doc IP/C/W/253 (2001).

South Asia Association for Regional Cooperation (SAARC), WT/L/326 of 22 October 1999.

Southern Africa Development Cooperation (SADC), WT/L/317 of 1 October 1999.

Standing Committee on the Law of Patents, Information Provided by Members of the Standing Committee on the Law of Patents (SCP) Concerning the Definition of Prior Art, WIPO Doc SCP/6/INF/2 (2001).

Statement of the Brazilian Delegation, in Report, Inter-governmental Committee on Intellectual Property and Genetic Resources, Traditional Knowledge and Folklore, 6th Session, Doc W1PO/GRTKF/IC/6/14 (2004).

Statements by New Zealand, Norway and the United States, in Report, Inter-governmental Committee on Intellectual Property and Genetic Resources, Traditional Knowledge and Folklore, Fourth Session, Doc WIPO/GRTKF/IC/4/15 (2002).

Suggestions for the Further Development of International Patent Law, Standing Committee on the Law of Patents, 4th Session, Geneva, November 2000, WIPO Doc SCP/4/2.

The Relationship Between the Convention on Biological Diversity (CBD) and the Agreement on the Trade-Related Aspects of Intellectual Property Rights (TRIPS): With a Focus on Article 27.3 (b), WTO Doc IP/C/W/175 (2000).

Traditional Knowledge—Selected Case Studies (Geneva: WIPO/UNEP, 2002).

WIPO, Basic Facts about the Patent Cooperation Treaty. The Worldwide System for Simplified Multiple Filing of Patent Applications, WIPO, April, 2002.

WIPO/UNEP, The Role of Intellectual Property Rights in the Sharing of Benefits Arising from the Use of Biological Resources and Associated.

WT/GC/W/23 of 5 July 1999.

WT/GC/W/251 of 13 July 1999.

WT/GC/W/282 of 6 August 1999.

WT/GC/W/302 of 6 August 1999.

WT/GC/W/362 of 12 October 1999.

WT/MIN(99)/3 of 2 November 1999.

Regional and Bilateral Treaties and Instruments

African Model Legislation for the Protection of Rights of Local Communities, Farmers, Breeders and for the Regulation of Access to Biological Resources, 2000.

Agreement between the EFTA States and Singapore, Egilsstadir, 26 June 2002.

Agreement between the EFTA States and the Hashemite Kingdom of Jordan, Vaduz, 21 June 2001.

Agreement between the Government of the United States of America and the Government of the Kingdom of Bahrain on the Establishment of a Free Trade Area, Washington, DC, 14 September 2004.

Agreement between the United States of America and the Hashemite Kingdom of Jordan on the Establishment of a Free Trade Area, Washington, 24 October 2000, 41 Int'l *Leg Mat* 63 (2002).

Agreement between the United States of America and the Lao Peoples Democratic Republic on Trade Relations, September 2003.

American Declaration of the Rights and Duties of Man, in United Nations, Human Rights—A Compilation of International Instruments, Vol. II, Regional Instruments, UN Doc ST/HR/1/Rev 5 (Vol. II) (1997).

United States, Morocco Free Trade Agreement, Washington, DC, 15 June 2004.

Statutes, Rules and Other

National Documents

Andean Community, Decision 486—Common Intellectual Property Regime, 14 September 2000.

Brazil, Industrial Property Law, Law No. 9.279 of 14 May 1996.

Brazil, Law No. 9456 (1997).

Brazil, Presidential Decree on Compulsory Licensing, Decree No 3,201, 6 October 1999.

Canada, Regulatory Directive Dir94-08: Assessment Criteria for Determining Environmental Safety of Plants with Novel Traits.

Costa Rica, Biodiversity Law, 1998.

India, Biological Diversity Act, 2002, Act 18 of 2003.

India, Biological Diversity Rules, 2003.

India, Department of Chemicals and Petrochemicals, Annual Report, 1999-2000.

India, Drug (Price Control) Order, 1995.

India, Geographical Indications of Goods (Registration and Protection) Act 1999, Act 48 of 1999.

India, Indian Council of Agricultural Research, Annual Report, 2002-03.

India, Joint Committee on the Protection of Plant Varieties and Farmers' Rights Bill, 1999, Report of the Joint Committee (2000).

India, Ministry of Finance, Economic Survey, 2003-04.

India, Parliament of India, The Patents (Second Amendment) Bill, 1999, Report of the Joint Committee, Notes of dissent (2001).

India, Patent (Amendment) Act, 2002.

India, Patents (Amendment) Act, 1999.

India, Patents Act, 1970.

India, Protection of Plant Varieties and Farmers' Rights Act, 2001, Act No. 53 of 2001, New Delhi : Universal Law Publishing Co. Pvt. Ltd.

India, Protection of Plant Varieties and Farmers' Rights Rules, 2003.

India, Rules for the Manufacture, Use, Import, Export and Storage of Hazardous Micro Organisms Genetically Engineered Organisms or Cells, 1989.

India, Seed Policy, 1988.

India, Trade Marks Act, 1999.

India, Indian Economic Survey, 2001-02 (2002).

Kenya, Seeds and Plant Varieties Act, Laws of Kenya, Chapter 326.

Norway, Act Relating to the Production and Use of Genetically Modified Organisms, 1993.

Panama, Ley No. 20 (del re'gimen especial de propiedad intelectual sobre los derechos colectivos de los pueblos indigenas), 2000.

Panama, Ministerio Comercio e Industrias, Decreto ejecutivo No. 12 (Por la cual se Reglamenta la Ley No. 20 de 26 de junio de 2000), 2001.

Peru, Law Introducing a Protection Regime for the Collective Knowledge of Indigenous Peoples Derived from Biological Resources, Law No. 27811, *Official Journal*, 10 August 2002.

Philippines, An Act to Recognise, Protect and Promote the Rights of Indigenous Cultural Communities/Indigenous

Peoples, Creating a National Commission on Indigenous Peoples, Establishing Implementing Mechanisms, Appropriating Funds Therefor, and for Other Purposes, 28 July 1997, Doc S No. 1728/H No. 9125.

Philippines, Executive Order No. 247 Prescribing Guidelines and Establishing a Regulatory Framework for the Prospecting of Biological and Genetic Resources, their By-Products and Derivatives, for Scientific and Commercial Purposes, and for Other Purposes, 18 May 1995.

Portugal, Decree-Law No. 118/2002, 20 April 2002.

South Africa, Medicines and Related Substances Control Amendment Act, 1997, Republic of South Africa, *Government Gazette,* 12 December 1997.

South Africa, National Environmental Management: Biodiversity Act, 2004.

Switzerland, Federal Law relating to Non-human Gene Technology, 2003, *Recueil Systimatique*-814.91.

Switzerland, Federal Law relating to the Protection of the Environment, 7 October 1983, *Recueil Systimatique,* 814.01.

Switzerland, Loi fed^rale sur les brevets d'invention, 25 June 1954, *Recueil officiel des lots fidiraks,* 1955, 893.

Switzerland, Projet de modification de la Loi sur la protection de Modification de la loi sur la protection de Penvironnement (LPE) [loi sur le genie g&ietique, LGG], Report of 30 April 2001.

Switzerland, Science, Education and Culture Commission—Council of States (Switzerland), 00.008 e Projet Gen-Lex (droit de la responsabilite civile), Report of 27 August 2001.

Tenvironnement, *Feuille fidiraley* p. 2327 (2000).

Thailand, Plant Varieties Protection Act, BE 2542 (1999).

United States, Federal Food, Drug, and Cosmetic Act, PL 98-417 (S 1538), (1984).

United States, Generalised System of Preferences Renewal Act of 1984, 98 *Stat* 2948 (1984).

United States Official Gazette, April 21, 1987

United States, Omnibus Trade and Competitiveness Act of 1988, PL 100-418, 23 August 1988.

United States, Patent and Trademark Office, Utility Examination Guidelines, 66/4 *Federal Register* 1092 (2001).

United States, Plant Patent Act of 1930, 35 USC 161 et seq.

United States, Trade Representative, *Special 301 Report* (2001-2004), United States, Uruguay Round Agreements Act, PL 103-46J), 8 December 1994.

Venezuela, Ley de diversidad biokSgica, 1999.

Journals

All India Reporter
Bioscience
Canadian Biotechnology
Casrip Newsletter
Economic and Political Weekly
Genet
Grain
Idea: The Journal of Law and Technology
Indian Bar Review
Indian Economic Survey
Indiana Journal of Global Legal Studies
International Affairs
Journal for Scientific and Industrial Research
Journal of Intellectual Property Rights
Journal of Patent Associated Literature
Official Journal European Patent Organisation
Pharmalicensing
Productivity
Science
Span
Supreme Court Cases
Supreme Court Journal
The Asia Pacific Journal of Environmental Law
The Company Law Journal
The Economist
The Frontline Magazine

The Journal of Indian Law Institute
The Journal of Law and Technology
The Journal of World Intellectual Property
The Journal of The US Department of Agriculture Economics Research Service
Washington University Journal of Law and Policy
Yojana

Newspapers

National Herald, New Delhi, 9th June 2003
The Hindu Daily, New Delhi Edition, Sept. 11, 2000, p. BS-4
The Hindu Daily, Feb. 22, 2001, B5-4
The Hindu Daily, March 8, 2001, p. BS-3
The Hindu Daily, March 8, 2001, B5-4
The Hindu, 22 March 2000
The Hindu, dt. 10th June, 1999 and January 5, 2004

Index